A HANDBOOK OF CIVIL WAR BULLETS AND CARTRIDGES

by
James E. Thomas & Dean S. Thomas

THOMAS PUBLICATIONS
Gettysburg, PA 17325

Front cover photo "Vicinity of Fort Steadman, Petersburg, Va."
courtesy of the Library of Congress.

ISBN-0-939631-94-6

CONTENTS

INTRODUCTION

When many Civil War collectors started in "the hobby," invariably they had a bullet collection. Bullets, and cartridges, were relatively inexpensive— and still are. But as the collector "advanced" to guns, uniforms, photographs, or accoutrements, the bullet collections ended up in cigar boxes in the basement. With the prices of all Civil War memorabilia steadily increasing, many collectors are returning to their bullets. This is not to say that the cost of bullets and cartridges has not risen, but compared to other artifacts, this area is still open to "beginners" with a limited budget. This book is intended for the growing number of bullet and cartridge collectors as a source of accurate information on bullets, cartridges, and their manufacturers. It can also be used as a guide and checklist to help build a collection.

Between 1948 and 1975, five books were compiled that are of importance to Civil War bullet and cartridge collectors: *Cartridges: a pictorial digest of small arms ammunition* by Herschel C. Logan; *Small Arms and Ammunition in the United States Service, 1776-1865* by Berkeley R. Lewis; *Bullets Used In the Civil War* by Stanley S. Phillips; and *Civil War Projectiles I* and *II* by M. E. Mason, Jr. and W. Reid McKee. These books have helped many of us to identify the pieces in our collections and the latter publication is still used by some as a standard reference. However, all of these books contain their share of misinformation and misidentifications, even though the authors took educated guesses when naming a bullet, its place of manufacture, or its intended weapon. Based on research done in the past twenty-five years, we hope to correct some of these errors.

In this book we have attempted to illustrate, as much as possible, the variety of Civil War small arms ammunition. Bullets and cartridges are listed and followed by any additional information. A series of measurements follows: "D" is the outside diameter of the bullet in inches, "L" is the length in inches, and "W" is the weight in grains. Any important variations are either shown or mentioned. Slight differences in the shape of a bullet's nose, rings, or the depth of the cavity are numerous and should for the most part simply be considered as minor differences found from mould to mould.

BACKGROUND

Ammunition for Civil War small arms was more varied than the weapons themselves. The period of the early 1860s was one of great ammunition development (the Minie ball was less than ten years old). Patentees constantly bombarded ordnance officers with new bullet and cartridge ideas for standard arms.

Weapon inventors and manufacturers (particularly of carbines and pistols) were inclined to make guns that required special, often patented, cartridges. These proprietary rounds were usually not made at the government arsenals and would therefore require the ordnance authorities to place orders for ammunition as well, if the arms were approved. Some of these inventions were worthless; however, others had merit and after testing were introduced into the ordnance pipelines.

A third reason for the great variety of ammunition was the fact that neither the North nor the South had a central laboratory or arsenal for fabricating small arms ammunition. Although the Confederacy made an effort with their facility at Macon, Georgia, the war did not last long enough for this to be fully accomplished. In the North, it does not appear that a central establishment was even considered. So even with strict regulations and guidelines, the Federal and Northern state arsenals and the smaller Confederate arsenals and depots often made different cartridges and bullets for the same arms. In addition to this, the bullet and cartridge requirements were supplemented by purchases from private manufacturers and abroad.

Civil War small arms ammunition ran the gamut from simple to complex. Although it was possible to load most weapons with loose powder and ball, this was seldom necessary except in the case of some non-standard weapons that soldiers brought from home. Both the Union and Confederate ordnance departments were more than able to supply the needs of their troops in the field. Any spotty shortages were more a matter of logistics than manufacturing shortfalls.

BULLETS

Civil War bullets were manufactured in several different ways. Casting was the least satisfactory method of forming a bullet. It required that the lead and mould both be extremely hot to prevent layering and air bubble entrapment which impaired the accurate flight of the bullet.

Prior to the introduction of the elongated expanding ball into the United States service, round balls had been made at several U.S. arsenals by machines using pressure or compression. "Balls thus made are more uniform in size and weight, smoother, more solid, and give more accurate results, than cast balls." In 1854, with the adoption by the U.S. Army of the "minnie" ball, a machine for their production was ordered to be constructed at the Allegheny Arsenal in Pittsburgh. By 1863 at least one of these or similar machines was in operation at the Benicia, Calif., Frankford (Philadelphia), St. Louis, Washington, Watervliet, N.Y., and Allegheny arsenals. To operate them the lead was first cast into round cylindrical bars and then rolled to a length of twenty-five inches. These bars were fed to the machine, which cut off a part sufficient for one ball and transferred it to a die in which the ball was formed, with cavity and rings.

The die was in two pieces, similar to a mould, and was operated by cams. A punch formed the cavity in the base of the bullet and at the same time forced the slug of lead into all the crevices of the die, the surplus metal being forced out in a thin belt around the ball in the direction of its axis. The die opened, the bullet dropped out, the die again closed and was ready to receive the next slug of lead. The balls were trimmed by hand, with a knife, and were then passed through a gauge of the proper size.

An English variation of the above method, for the manufacture of the Enfield bullet, involved the use of a one piece die and two punches. One punch, with a conical indentation, actually became a part of the die and formed a portion of the nose of the bullet during compression. The other punch acted, as in the American method, to form the ball with its cavity in the base. After the second punch was withdrawn, the first pushed the bullet out of the die in the direction in which the second had exited, then returned to its prior position.

Another method of bullet manufacture was "pressed and turned." These machines took a lead slug and pressed it to form the nose and the cavity. The partially formed ball was then transported to an automatic lathe where a cutting tool formed the grooves and finished the bullet as it spun. A machine of this type was put in operation at Frankford Arsenal in 1862.

One final observation of Civil War ammunition involves the actual diameter of bullets and the nominal caliber of weapons. Muzzleloaders had to use bullets that were smaller than the bore diameter, in order for the weapon to be loaded properly. Therefore, the .58 caliber M1861 Springfield rifle musket used a bullet .574 inches in diameter. Breechloading carbines and rifles, and revolvers used bullets larger than the bore diameter. Thus, the bullet for the .52 caliber Sharps carbine or rifle was actually .535 inches in diameter, and a .44 caliber Colt bullet was .455 inches in diameter. Packages and crates are sometimes marked with the bore diameter of the weapon and at other times with the diameter of the ammunition.

CARTRIDGES

The most common ammunition used with muzzleloaders during the war was the paper wrapped cartridge. Here, the bullet and powder charge were encased in paper, and it required that the soldier open the round to pour the powder down the barrel. Federal procedures demanded that the bullet be completely void of paper before it was rammed home; however, some Confederate and imported cartridges of this type were lubricated at the bullet end and were intended to be loaded still wrapped in the cartridge.

Combustible cartridges fall into the category of separate primed ammunition that saw extensive use with carbines and revolvers. A combustible cartridge had the bullet attached to a cartridge case made of thin nitrated paper, linen, membrane, collodion or other substance that would be completely consumed by the powder charge explosion. It did not need to be opened to expose the powder, and was ignited by the flame from a regular percussion cap. Several combustible cartridges were adapted for use in muzzleloaders.

Other than the combustible cartridges, most separate primed cartridges were best suited for breechloading carbines and rifles, and were an important factor in sustaining an increased rate of fire. Generally, besides the combustible varieties, this type of cartridge had a case made of copper or brass, or brass and paper, or India rubber. The flame from the percussion cap penetrated through a small hole in the base of the case and ignited the powder charge. Unfortunately, many of these "spent" cases were difficult to remove from the breech of the gun.

The most advanced types of ammunition used during the war were those that were internally primed, such as the rimfire, pin-fire, and certain evasions of Smith and Wesson's rimfire patent. The rimfire cartridge was completely self-contained: it had together in one piece the primer, powder, bullet, and case. The cartridge cases went through at least eight steps in the forming process before they were ready to be charged with fulminate, which was "spun" into the outer recesses of the "rim" at the base of the case. After the appropriate powder charge was inserted, the bullet was crimped into the open end of the case. In operation, the hammer of the gun struck the rim of the cartridge, igniting the fulminate and in turn the powder charge. An earlier development that saw limited use in this country was the pin-fire cartridge. Here, a stout, brass wire "pin" protruded through the side of the case. When struck by the hammer, the pin was driven into percussion compound that rested on an anvil. The resulting explosion ignited the powder charge.

Cartridges were packaged by the arsenals and manufacturers in many assorted ways. Generally, ammunition made at arsenals for muzzleloaders was put up in paper wrapped bundles of ten cartridges. Confederate wrappers are usually marked with the type of cartridge and place and date of manufacture. Regrettably, Union ammunition is not similarly identified, except on wooden packing crates for 1,000 rounds. Other methods of wrapping cartridges by private makers varied from pasteboard boxes to paper covered, drilled wooden blocks. The number of revolver cartridges in a package usually corresponded to the number of chambers in the weapon's cylinder.

IGNITION

Ignition, in reference to small arms, is the method or means used to explode the powder charge. Generally speaking, Civil War era ammunition was ignited in one of three different ways: flint and steel, percussion primers, or internally primed cartridges.

Flint and Steel. This method was outdated long before the Civil War, but the need for serviceable arms at the onset brought many flintlock guns out of storage before they could be altered to the newer percussion system. This system employed a piece of flint and a piece of steel called a frizzen. The frizzen served a dual purpose: when not being actively used, it was a cover for a small "pan" that contained a priming charge of about ten grains of black powder. In operation, when the flint struck the frizzen, the frizzen snapped back exposing the priming charge at the same time a shower of sparks fell into the pan. The sparks ignited the priming charge and passed fire through a small hole in the side of the barrel that communicated with the main powder charge in the barrel.

Percussion Primers. The principal means of ignition in Civil War small arms was the percussion system that used the copper percussion cap. The cap looked like a tiny "top hat" and was about the size of a modern pencil eraser. Pistol caps were usually straight-sided without the "brim" and were smaller still. The interior of the percussion cap had a small deposit of fulminate of mercury. The correct formula produced a substance that exploded when it was struck a sharp blow. After loading the weapon, a percussion cap was placed by hand onto a hollow tube, called a cone or nipple, at the breech end of the barrel. When the hammer was tripped it fell onto the percussion cap. The exploding cap shot a concentrated flame into the barrel or a chamber and ignited the powder charge. In the Federal service twelve percussion caps were packaged in each bundle of ten cartridges; for quality reasons, the Confederates usually packaged thirteen caps. Each round or charge to be fired needed a new cap.

Methods to improve on the percussion cap began soon after its adoption by the United States in the early 1840s. Edward Maynard was issued a patent for his percussion tape primers on September 22, 1845. The invention, very similar to present-day rolls of caps for toy guns, was purchased by the U.S. Ordnance Department for use with its Model of 1855 arms, and other weapons were altered for its employment. In Maynard's idea, small pellets of fulminate were cemented between two strips of paper and then shellacked for moisture resistance. A coil of forty primers was placed in a special compartment in the lockplate and were fed out over the cone one at a time by cocking the hammer. The lockplate and hammer were so arranged that when the hammer was tripped it cut off the exposed primer from the strip and ignited it on the cone. Although the Maynard tape primers themselves cost only 33 cents per thousand to manufacture at the Frankford Arsenal in 1859, the Civil War emergency created the Model of 1861 rifle musket that was quicker and cheaper to make than the M1855 because it eliminated the Maynard primer mechanism. By mid-May 1861, Federal arsenals were ordered to no longer issue tape primers and to package only percussion caps with their ammunition.

On June 28, 1853, Christian Sharps, of Sharps carbine and rifle fame, was issued a patent for an improved percussion "disc" primer that was adapted to the small arms of his name. The primer was made of two thin copper discs that encased a fulminate charge. About twenty-five primers were packaged with a wooden spacer in an open-sided brass sleeve. The spacer served to push the primers into a special mechanism or magazine located behind the breech and on top of the lockplate of several models. Hammer action ejected one disc at a time just in time to be crushed and exploded on the weapon's cone. A later modification to the mechanism allowed the magazine to be "cut-off" so the user could employ regulation percussion caps while the magazine remained in reserve. The Federal government purchased only about 2,000,000 Sharps primers at various times during the Civil War.

Internally Primed Cartridges. The most advanced form of ignition used in Civil War weapons was the internally primed cartridge. Here the primer, powder charge and bullet were combined in one unit or cartridge that was virtually impervious to moisture. A soldier was not required to prime the weapon with loose powder or handle a separate small primer. The gun could be quickly loaded in one motion and thus the rate of fire was dramatically increased. Two kinds of internally primed cartridges, the rimfire and pinfire, have been previously discussed. A third kind worth mentioning was a primitive form of the modern centerfire. On June 29, 1858, George Washington Morse of Baton Rouge, Louisiana was issued a patent for an improvement in cartridges that had all the features of an internally primed cartridge. Morse devised a hollow copper or brass cartridge case with an "anvil" secured inside near the base. A standard percussion cap was placed on the anvil and the base was sealed with a rubberized "donut" leaving the flat portion of the cap exposed. The prepared case was charged with powder and a bullet inserted in the open end. Basically, a "firing pin" in the breech of the weapon was driven forward by the hammer. When the pin struck the center of the cartridge it exploded the cap and in turn the powder charge. It was claimed that the cases were reusable. The U.S. Ordnance Department was impressed enough with the system to have trial guns and ammunition prepared, but before any conclusive tests were done the Civil War began. Morse sided with the Confederacy and soon developed a new breechloading carbine for his ammunition. Perhaps as many as 1,000 carbines were produced during the war at various locations in the South. The weapon and its unique cartridges saw limited use, but are known to have been used in the Battle of Bentonville, North Carolina and elsewhere.

Finally, an excellent website exists at http://civilwarprojectiles.com for those interested in Civil War ammunition. This site hosts feature articles, reference tools, and a web forum. Many collectors from across the country are available there to identify bullets and answer questions about small arms and artillery.

.22 TO *.44* CALIBER FOR PISTOLS

Bullets from .22 to .44 caliber generally represent ammunition for revolvers and single shot pistols.

Revolver bullets share two common characteristics. They have a solid base and are a larger diameter than the bore of their intended weapon. Revolvers were, in essence, breechloaders with the bullets being fired from the cylinder into and through the barrel.

Sharps pattern bullets of these calibers are NOT included in this section, Sharps bullets of all calibers are in their own section.

| 1A | B | 2 | 3 | 4 | 5 | 6 |

1   **6MM and 9MM, Flobert** — Louis Flobert of Paris, France, developed the "bulleted breech cap" in the 1840s. These are the predecessors of the .22 rimfire. No headstamp.
     Cartridges: **A** - D .228, L .37, W 17   **B** - D .345, L .60, W 86

2   **.22 cal., Smith & Wesson** — Self-contained rimfire cartridge. No headstamp.   *Cartridge: D .235, L .70*

3   **.28 cal.** — Solid bullet with a raised band. For "pocket" revolver.
     Bullet: D .285, L .40, W 47

4   **.28 cal.** — Common Colt profile with rebated base. Cartridge made of untreated paper and glued to the bullet. For "pocket" revolver.
     Bullet: D .283, L .43, W 52   Cartridge: L 1.23

5   **.31 cal.** — Bullet and cartridge construction same type as #4. For "pocket" revolver.
     Bullet: D .320, L .48, W 76   Cartridge: L .99

6   **.31 cal.** — Shorter variant of #5. For "pocket" revolver.
     Bullet: D .325, L .42, W 68

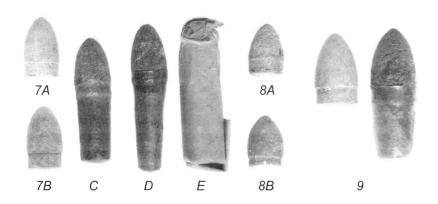

7A   8A

7B   C   D   E   8B   9

7   **.36 cal.** — For "Navy," "police" and "belt" revolvers. "A" is a solid bullet with rebated base. "B" is a variant — machine pressed with a punch-hole in the base.

Cartridge "C" with the case pasted to the bullet was manufactured by Robert Chadwick *(L 1.26)*. "D" is a patented combustible cartridge made by Johnston & Dow (see also #47) *(L 1.49)*. "E" was made in the typical "American military" or "regulation" style, i.e., powder charge and bullet wrapped completely in paper, tied over the nose of the bullet, with the powder end being closed with folds which formed a tail. The manufacturer of these was probably the Frankford Arsenal *(L 1.48)*.

     Bullet: *A - D .378, L .62, W 141*   *B - D .384, L .627, W 142*

8   **.36 cal.** — Two shorter variants of #7.
     Bullets: *A - D .374, L .53, W 109*   *B - D .388, L .53, W 119*

9   **.44 cal., Elam O. Potter** — For "Army" and "holster" revolvers. Solid bullet with rebated base. The cartridge was made under Johnston & Dow's patent by Elam O. Potter.
     Bullet: D .452, L .73, W 229   *Cartridge: L 1.32*

10   **.44 cal., Watervliet Arsenal** — Solid bullet with rebated base. These are slightly taller than #9. A machine pressed variant of "A" exists with a small punch-hole in the base. "B" features serrations around the rebated base. The cartridge was made by pasting an untreated paper case to the ball.
     Bullets: A - D .455, L .78, W 253   *B - D .456, L .802, W 264*
     Cartridge: L 1.36

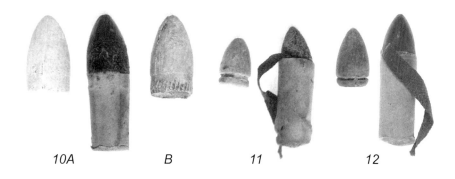

10A   B   11   12

11   **.31 cal., Eley** — Solid bullet with one groove. A knife cut is often visible where the cartridge case material was trimmed. Skin cartridge made by Eley Bros., London. Protective outer wrapper of paper with a cloth tearstrip. An Eley label (orange or blue) is often on the bottom of the outer case. See also #12, 18, 24, 45.
Bullet: D .323, L .49, W 78   Cartridge: L 1.24

12   **.36 cal., Eley** — Solid bullet with one groove, knife cut and rounded base. Cartridge and wrapper by Eley Bros.
Bullet: D .386, L .622, W 130   Cartridge: L 1.390

13   **.32 cal., Smith & Wesson** — Solid bullet with two grooves. A third groove is often present where the bullet was crimped into the copper case. Self-contained rimfire cartridge. No headstamp.
Bullet: D .320; L .50; W 73   Cartridge: L 1.23

14   **.40 cal., Derringer** — Solid bullet, two grooves and crimp mark. Rimfire cartridge manufactured by C.D. Leet. No headstamp.
Bullet: D .400, L .55, W 121   Cartridge: L .94

13   14   15A   B

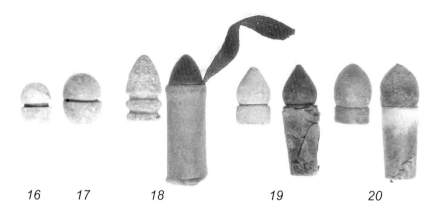

16   17   18   19   20

15   **.31 and .41 cal., Volcanic** — Volcanic bullets are actually self-contained cartridges. Smith & Wesson held the patent (#14,147 dated January 22, 1856) for these bullets. There are many variations found in the rings and the bases. Primers in the bases were sealed with combinations of cork, brass, and iron.
Bullets: ***A*** *- D .355, L 58, W 54*   ***B*** *- D .453, L .70, W 111*

16   **.31 cal., Walch** — Cast bullet with one deep groove. Walch 12-shot revolvers were made by J.P. Lindsay. These unusual pistols had an extra long cylinder that held two loads in each chamber. The deep groove in the ball contained lubricant to seal the chamber between the loads thus eliminating the danger of chain-fire.
Bullet: D .326, L .41, W 64

17   **.36 cal., Walch.**   *Bullet: D .385, L .51, W 123*

18   **.36 cal., Eley** — Solid base, two grooves. See also #11, 24, 45.
Bullet: D .379, L .67, W 137   *Cartridge: L 1.3*

19   **.36 cal., Richmond Laboratory** — This odd looking bullet has a solid base and one groove. Cast at the Richmond Laboratory.
Bullet: D .368, L .58, W 117   *Cartridge: L 1.12*

20   **.36 cal.** — Confederate manufacture. Very similar to #19.
Bullet: D .413, L .60, W 150   *Cartridge: L 1.16*

21   **.40 cal., LeMat** — Solid bullet, one groove, two variations. The nine-shot LeMat revolver also had a smoothbore barrel that fired buckshot. The buckshot cartridges are extremely rare *(L 2.17)*. The Confederacy produced LeMat cartridges at Richmond.
Bullets: ***A*** *- D .413, L .62, W 166*   ***B*** *- D .413, L .65, W 169.*
Cartridge: L 1.00

21A   B   22

22   **.40 cal.** — Bullet is similar to the LeMat, but cartridge construction suggests European manufacture.

Bullet: D .414, L .64, W 146   Cartridge: L 1.14

23   **.31, .36, and .44 cal., Deane & Adams** — The pin on these bullets was designed to hold a wad. This bullet and associated copper "dustbin" cartridge was developed by Robert Adams in England in the early 1850s.

*Bullets: **A** - D .337, L .65, W 85   **B** - D .405, L .64, W 100*
*   **C** - D .434, L .76, W 159   **D** - D .462, L .75, W 201*

24   **.36 and .44 cal., Tranter** — Solid base with one wide, deep groove. For Tranter revolvers imported by the South. Cartridge and wrapper by Eley Bros.

*Bullets: **A** - D .395, L .50, W 120   **B** - D .450, L .59, W 176*
Cartridge: L 1.07

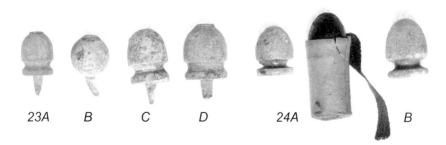

23A   B   C   D   24A   B

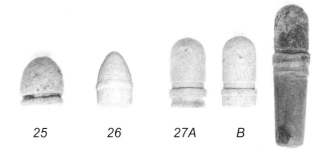

25   26   27A   B

25   **.44 cal.** — Solid base with one narrow groove. Similar to Tranter.
     Bullet: D .455, L .50, W 166

26   **.36 cal., Colt** — Solid bullet with a raised band. See specimen #3 for similarities.
     Bullet: D .395, L .561, W 130

27   **.36 cal., Savage** — Solid base, round nose bullet with one wide groove. Additionally, "A" has a second, round groove at the bottom while "B" features a rebated base. The cartridge of untreated paper (shown) was made by Robert Chadwick. Skin cartridges (not shown) made up with Savage bullets were manufactured by D.C. Sage (see #40 below).
     *Bullets: **A** - D .388, L .707, W 177   **B** - D .380, L .71, W 179*
     Cartridge: L 1.43

28   29   30   31

28   **.36 cal., Colt** — Solid bullet with one groove and a rebated base. The cartridge case was made of paper impregnated with saltpeter to ensure that it was entirely consumed.
     Bullet: D .382, L .55, W 121   Cartridge: L 1.21

29   **.36 cal., Colt** — Variant of #28 with tapered edge around base and noticeable sprue. Made by H.W. Mason after the Civil War.
     Bullet: D .380, L .69, W 130

30 **.36 cal., Bartholow** — Another variant of #28 with punch-hole in base. See also #48.

Bullet: D .385, L .62, W 140   Cartridge: L 1.078

31 **.36 cal., Hazard** — Bullet similar to #28. Cartridges were made by the Hazard Powder Company under Doremus & Budd's patents #34,725 & #34,744 dated March 18 & 25, 1862. The powder charge was moulded by pressure into a cake which was then attached to the bullet and waterproofed with collodion or shellac.

Bullet: D .387, L .61, W 145   Cartridge: L 1.18

32 **.44 cal., Colt Army** — Colt's "New Model" bullet with a solid base, one groove, and rebated base.

Bullet: D .455, L .67, W 196

33 **.44 cal.** — These cartridges used the same bullet (#32) but were from different manufacturers. Cartridge "A" is from the Hazard Powder Company, see also #31. "B" was probably made by Colt and is untreated paper pasted to the bullet. Cartridge "C" was made in the "regulation" style at an arsenal, see also #7E.

Cartridges: A - L 1.25   B - L 1.88   C - L 1.30

34 **.44 cal., Colt** — Made by H.W. Mason, see #29.

Bullet: D .461, L .70, W 216

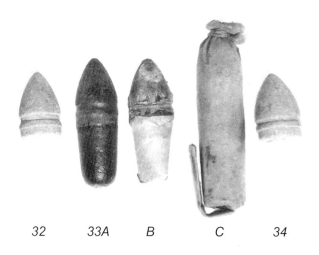

32   33A   B   C   34

35

35 **.44 cal., Richmond Colt** — Bullet similar to #32 but with less definition of the rebated base. A knife cut is often visible in the groove where the paper cartridge case was trimmed. Made at the Richmond Laboratory.

Bullet: D .455, L .67, W 201   *Cartridge: L 1.28*

36A   *B*   *37*

36 **.31 and .36 cal., Hayes** — Two-groove, solid bullets. "A" is the .31 caliber cartridge shown without the protective wrapper. Note thread around case. "B" is the .36 bullet and cartridge. Robert Hayes of the Royal Navy received English patent #2,059 dated September 4, 1856, for a cartridge case made of animal intestines. This was then strengthened by winding thread around the case. The cartridge was then packaged in a protective envelope with a tear strip and label. Labels are seen in white and blue.

Bullet: D .386, L .62, W 135
*Cartridges: **A** - L 1.00   **B** - L 1.40*

37 **.44 cal., Hayes.** *Bullet: D .448, L .64, W 204*   *Cartridge: L 1.3*

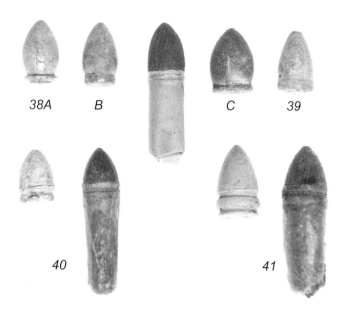

38A   B   C   39

40   41

38   **.36 cal., St. Louis Arsenal** — Unusual shaped bullet with one groove at the base. A sprue is often visible on base. Untreated paper cartridge tied to the bullet and closed with folded tail. These St. Louis Arsenal cartridges have been mistakenly attributed to "Remington" and "Leech & Rigdon" by collectors in the past. "C" is a similar ball in .44 caliber but of unknown origin.

     Bullets: **A** *D .385, L .64, W 135*   **B** *D .383, L .62, W 134*
              C *D .450, L .64, W 201*   *Cartridge: L 1.40*

39   **.36 cal.** — Shallow square groove, base cast. Unknown origin.

     Bullet: D .380, L .64, W 128

40   **.36 cal., Sage** — Ball has one groove and a solid base. Knife cuts are usually visible where the case material was trimmed. "Seamless" cartridges manufactured by D.C. Sage were made under Hotchkiss' patent (#34,367, Feb. 11, 1862). Strips of mutton or hog's intestine was spirally wound around a former so that the seams crossed perpendicular to each other in order to form a seamless cartridge case. The case was filled with powder and tied to the bullet with thread.

     Bullet: D .380, L .53, W 117   *Cartridge: L 1.46*

41   **.44 cal., Sage** — Two groove bullet with rounded band between grooves. Knife cut visible.

     Bullet: D .458, L .74, W 215   *Cartridge: L 1.49*

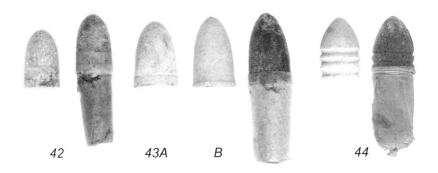

42   43A   B   44

42   **.36 cal., Starr** — Solid bullet with a raised band around base. Cartridges consisted of untreated paper pasted to the bullets.
   Bullet: D .387, L .59, W 140   Cartridge: L 1.31

43   **.44 cal., Starr** — Note difference in the height of the raised band on these two specimens. See also #94.
   *Bullets: **A** - D .469, L .68, W 221   **B** - D .461, L .73, W 223*
   Cartridge: L 1.50

44   **.44 cal.** — Solid bullet, three round grooves, the bottom groove used as a "tie ring." Possibly for the Joslyn revolver.
   Bullet: D .455, L .66, W 212   Cartridge: L 1.445

45A   B   46   47

45   **.44 cal., Kerr** — Solid base, two grooves. "A" has a pointy nose. "B" has a round nose and tapered base. The cartridge was made by Eley Bros. London.
   *Bullets: **A** - D .465, L .72, W 224   **B** - D .455, L .660, W 205*
   Cartridge: L 1.21

46 **.44 cal., Leet & Hall** — Solid bullet with two round grooves. Made by Leet & Hall under Julius Hotchkiss' patent, see #40.

Bullet: D .460, L .67, W 216   Cartridge: L 1.51

47 **.44 cal., Johnston and Dow** — A similar bullet to #32 above, the difference being a much longer rebated base. Johnston & Dow received patent #33,393, #34,061, and #35,687 dated October 1, 1861, January 7, and June 24, 1862, for their cartridges. Using paper or fabric that was treated to make it combustible, the cartridge case was pasted to the bullet and was then covered with collodion to make it waterproof.

Bullet: D .464, L .69, W 207   Cartridge: L 1.67

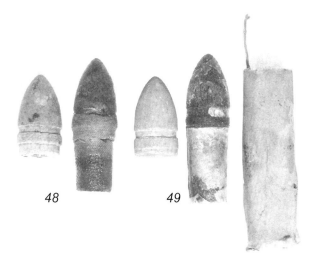

48   49

48 **.44 cal., Bartholow** — Bullet with one groove, rebated base and a small punch-hole in the base. Roberts Bartholow received patent #36,066 dated August 5, 1862 for his cartridges which consisted of a pressed powder cylinder glued to the bullet. A characteristic of Bartholow cartridges of any caliber is a silk strip that was added to reinforce the joint between the bullet and the powder.

Bullet: D .458, L .81, W 253   Cartridge: L 1.24

49 **.44 caliber, Colt** — "Old Model" bullet with similar profile to #48, but with a solid base. The cartridge case is of paper and pasted to the bullet. Packaged in paper tube with tear string.

Bullet: D .460, L .79, W 256   Cartridge: L 1.48

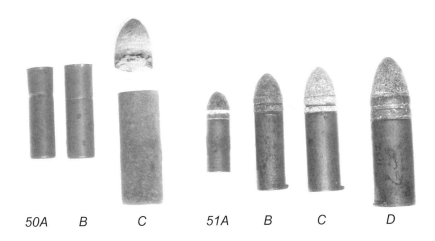

50A   B   C   51A   B   C   D

50   **.26, .28, .39 caliber, cupfire** — Willard Ellis and John White patented this cartridge (#24,726 dated July 12, 1859) in an attempt to avoid Smith and Wesson's rimfire patent. The cartridge operated in the same manner as the rimfire, the difference being where the fulminate was held. For use in the Plant revolver.

Bullet: D .390, L .50, W 111
Cartridges: ***A*** *- L .92*   ***B*** *- L .94*   ***C*** *- L 1.11*

51   **.25, .32, .36, and .44 caliber, lip fire** — The Allen bullet is distinctive with its two raised bands. Ethan Allen received patent #30,109 dated September 25, 1860 for the lip fire cartridge. The small "lip" on the bottom of the cartridge case contained the fulminate. Made for the Allen & Wheelock revolver.

Cartridges: ***A*** *- L .82*   ***B*** *- L 1.18*   ***C*** *- L 1.25*   ***D*** *- L 1.50*

52   **.32 and .45 caliber, teatfire** — David Williamson received patent #41,183 dated January 5, 1864, for this cartridge. The teat at the end of the cartridge held the fulminate. Originally the cartridges were made with a flat teat which was later modified to a round teat to simplify loading. For use in the Moore revolver.

Cartridges: ***A*** *- L 1.26*   ***B*** *- L 1.52*

53   **9mm and 12 mm, pinfire** — Pinfires were another example of a self-contained cartridge. The "pin" rests in a percussion cap seated in the bottom of the case. When struck by the pistol hammer, the pin exploded the cap igniting the powder charge.

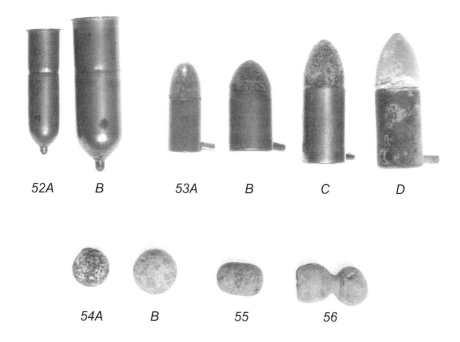

52A   B   53A   B   C   D

54A   B   55   56

Pinfire cartridges were primarily made in Europe and were measured in millimeters. Cartridge "B" was made in Europe and is marked, "Fusnot • Bruxelles." "H • B Paris" (Houllier and Blanchard, Paris) is the headstamp for another commonly found maker. However Ethan Allen "C" and C.D. Leet "D" did make 12mm pinfire cartridges during the Civil War period.

Pin fire cartridges were also made in 2mm (blanks for watchfob pistols), 5mm, 7mm, 15mm, and for shotguns. Of these probably only the 9mm and 12mm saw military service.

*Cartridges: **A** - L .972   **B** - L .94   **C** - L 1.24   **D** - L 1.35*

54   **.36 and .44 cal., Round ball.**
    *Bullets: **A** - D .413, W 103   **B** - D .464, W 138*

55   **.36 cal.** — Called a double-ended shot.
    Bullet: D .335, L .49, W 91

56   **.44 cal., "Bar-shot."** — This was cast in a crude mould and was probably meant to be cut in half. There is also a possibility that these are not even bullets. They may be C.S. bayonet scabbard finials.

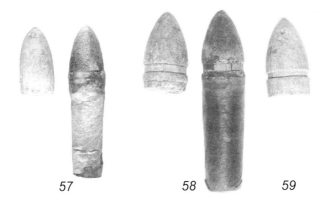

57   58   59

57   **.36 cal., Colt revolving rifle** — Solid bullet with rebated base. Looks like a tall variant of #7. Cartridge is of treated paper.
Bullet: D .383, L .702, W 161   Cartridge: L 1.589

58   **.44 cal., Colt revolving rifle** — Colt "old model" bullet. The cartridge is constructed the same as for pistols but contains a larger powder charge for the rifle. See also #84 and #96.
Bullet: D .462, L .81, W 258   Cartridge: L 1.82

59   **.44 cal.** — Variant of above. The tapered base (not rebated) and knife cut suggest southern manufacture. See #35 and #92.
Bullet: D .459, L .80, W 258

60

60   **.44 cal., Henry** — Self-contained rimfire cartridge for Henry rifle. "B" has a blunt nose bullet. "H" headstamps are common.
Bullet: D .445, L .67, W 209   Cartridges: A - L 1.35   B - L 1.07

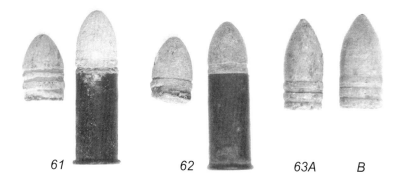

61   62   63A   B

61   **.44 cal., Ballard** — Self-contained rimfire cartridge for Ballard "new model" carbine or rifle.

Bullet: D .434, L .67, W 205   Cartridge: L 1.53

62   **.42 cal., Wesson** — Self-contained rimfire cartridge.

Bullet: D .432, L .68, W 185   Cartridge: L 1.48

63   **.44 cal., Tennessee Rifle** — Both have cone cavities with teats in the base. For "Kentucky" or "country" rifles bored or re-rifled to approximately .44 caliber by the state of Tennessee.

*Bullets: **A** - D .425, L .92, W 222   **B** - D .450, L .93, W 271*

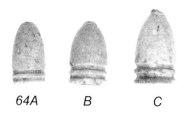

64A   B   C

64   **.355, .405 and .445 dia., Tennessee Rifle** — Two-grooved coni-cal ball with cone cavity. Probably for "Tennessee" or similar small bore rifles. See also #85. One document shows that some Tennessee rifle balls were ordered by weight instead of by cali-ber; i.e., "50 to the pound," which is approximately 140 grains, see 64-b.

*Bullets: **A** - D .355, L .62, W 108   **B** - D .405, L .64, W 140*
*   **C** - D .445, L .74, W 195*

65   66   67   68

65   **.45 cal., Whitworth** — Cast cylindrical bullet with cone cavity. The English Whitworth was a sharpshooters rifle. Only the Confederacy imported Whitworth rifles.
Bullet: D .445, L 1.40, W 515

66   **.45 cal., Whitworth** — Machine pressed bullet with a "42" in the cavity. This specimen would have been machine pressed in England. Excavated near Gettysburg.
Bullet: D .442, L 1.38, W 516

67   **.45 cal., Whitworth** — Fired cylindrical specimen displaying hexagonal shape of the barrel. The actual hex-shaped bullet for the Whitworth was probably not used in America during the war.
Bullet: D .450, L 1.28, W 516

68   **.45 cal.** — Solid "double-end" slug. This has been called a "double-end Whitworth." More recently it has been suggested that this could have been for the Vandenberg Volley gun. More research is needed.
Bullet: D .442, L 1.39, W 503

.45-70 Sharps — Previously believed to be Whitworths, these have since been identified as coming from post-Civil War Sharps metallic cartridges (1876-1880s). Dished base with dot in center. Long and short variants.

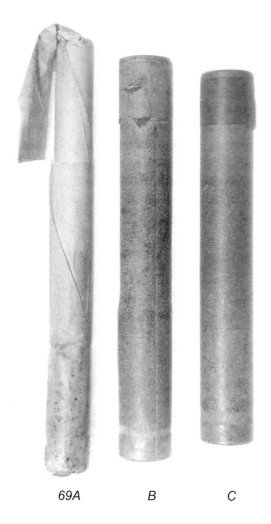

69A   B   C

69   **.45 cal., Whitworth** — Three examples of the English Whitworth cartridge. The rolled paper cartridge was made in England by Eley. The cardboard tube cartridge was patented in 1859 and was also of English manufacture.

*Cartridges: **A** - L 4.39; **B** - L 3.90; **C** - L 3.61*

26

.50 TO *.58* CALIBER FOR CARBINES AND RIFLES

The ammunition included in this section represents that used in carbines and rifles. As mentioned before, breechloading weapons used bullets of a larger diameter than the bore and typically have a solid base.

The variety of cartridge cases shown in this section illustrates the imagination of inventors who tried to remedy a serious flaw found in breechloading carbines. The challange was to create a case that would expand to seal the breech and eliminate the leak of gases during firing, while contracting enough afterwards to allow for the removal of the spent case.

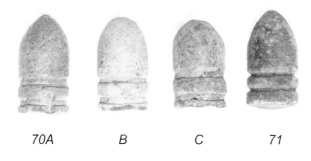

70A   B   C   71

70   **.50 cal.** — Confederate manufacture for unknown carbine, solid base with two square grooves, two variations. A third variant, "C" has a cone cavity and was probably for a .54 cal. muzzleloader.
Bullets: **A** *- D .515, L .95, W 443*   **B** *- D .518, L .91, W 437*
C *- D .534, L .86, W 348*

71   **.50 cal.** — Southern manufacture for unknown carbine. Similar in profile to #70, but with different grooves and a pronounced sprue "nip" on the bottom.
Bullet: D .515, L .95, W 398

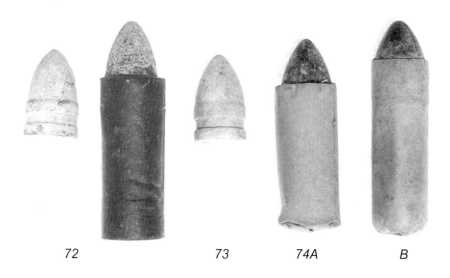

72   73   74A   B

72   **.50 cal., Smith** — Solid bullet with two raised bands. The "rubber case" cartridge was patented by Gilbert Smith (#17,702 dated June 30, 1857). The cartridge case was constructed of india-rubber cloth or vulcanized india-rubber. The base has a small perforation to allow the percussion cap flame to ignite the charge (separate primed).
Bullet: D .523, L .97, W 345   Cartridge: L 2.07

73   **.50 cal., Smith/Gallager** — Solid bullet with one flat groove. Used in Poultney's cartridges for Smith's and Gallager's carbine.
Bullet: D .524, L .86, W 360

74   **.50 cal., Smith/Gallager** — Cartridges containing bullet #73. These were manufactured under Poultney's patent. The patent (#40,988 dated December 15, 1863) was originally granted to Thomas Rodman and Silas Crispin who assigned it to Thomas Poultney. The cases were made of brass foil and paper with a perforation in the base. "A" is shaped to fit into the Smith carbine. "B" is longer and thinner and is shaped to fit into the Gallager.
*Cartridges: **A** - L 1.84   **B** - L 2.05*

75   **.50 cal., Gallager** — The bullets for the Gallagher cartridges made by Samuel Jackson somewhat resemble the regulation "minie." These bullets have cone cavities. Specimen "B" has

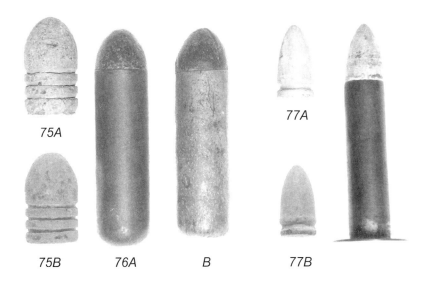

75A

75B   76A   B   77B

77A

six "spokes" in the base which were probably created by a center or punch during manufacture.

*Bullets: **A** - D .530, L .95, W 445   **B** - D .529, L .859, W 398*

76   .50 cal., Gallager — The cartridge case "A" is made of drawn brass and was separate primed. These were supplied to the Federal government by Richardson and Overman of Philadelphia but were manufactured by Samuel Jackson. A variant of this cartridge with a tinned brass case also exists. "B" was made of tinned iron wrapped in paper, for which Samuel Jackson held the patent (#45,830 dated January 10, 1865).

*Cartridges: **A** - L 2.08   **B** - L 2.01*

77   .36 cal., Maynard — "A" is the generic pattern with a solid base and one groove. "B" has a raised band above the groove and was cast in a Mass. Arms Co. mold. Dr. Edward Maynard held patent #22,565 dated January 11, 1859. By this patent, cartridge cases for the Maynard carbine were made of drawn brass to form a tube with a closed end. A brass disk was soldered to the base of the tube. The large diameter of the base disk was to aid in extracting the case after firing. The cartridge was separate primed — a small hole in the base allowed the flame from a percussion cap through to ignite the powder charge.

*Bullet: **A** - D .379, L .73, W 150   **B** - D .364, L .68, W 133*
Cartridge: L 2.11

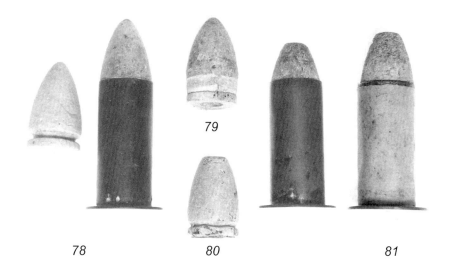

79

78   *80*   *81*

78   **.50 cal., Maynard** — The bullet has a solid base and one groove.
Bullet: D .525, L .88, W 342   Cartridge: L 1.82

79   **.50 cal., Maynard** — Variant, shallow cone cavity (0.14 deep).
Bullet: D .525, L .85, W 348

80   **.50 cal., Maynard** — Variant, rounded cavity (0.205 deep).
Bullet: D .518, L .78, W 331   Cartridge: L 1.58

81   **.50 cal., Maynard** — This cartridge was made by Thomas Poultney in the same fashion as #74.   *Cartridge: L 1.68*

82   **.50 cal., Morse** — Solid, two groove bullet with flat nose. George Morse held U.S. patent #20,727 dated June 29, 1858 for this reloadable carbine cartridge. These were manufactured at Greenville, SC. The case had a wire or "anvil" in the end on which sat the percussion cap. A gasket sealed the remaining open space around the cap. The case was filled with powder and a bullet was friction-fit into the end.
Bullet: D .525, L .835, W 330   Cartridge: L 2.08

83   **.50 cal., Warner** — Solid bullet, two grooves and crimp mark. Self-contained copper rimfire cartridge. Similar to the Spencer cartridge except for caliber. No headstamp.
Bullet: D .510, L .84, W 326   Cartridge: D .515, L 1.54

82   83   84

85   86   87   88

84   **.50 cal., Colt revolving rifle** — Two-grooves with a rebated base.
Bullet: D .500, L .88, W 346   Cartridge: L 1.91

85   **.52 cal.** — Confederate manufacture for muzzleloading carbine or rifle. Two grooves, cone cavity, see #64 for similarities.
Bullet: D .506, L .83, W 324

86   **.52 cal.** — Confederate manufacture for breechloading carbine. Solid bullet with rebated base. Sprue mark visible on the base.
Bullet: D .538, L .85, W 446

87 **.52 cal., Spencer** — Solid bullet, two grooves and crimp mark. Variations are found in the groove patterns since there were at least five companies making these cartridges. These were completely self-contained rimfire cartridges: bullet, powder, case, and primer in one piece. Made under Smith and Wesson's patent (#27,933 dated April 17, 1860), the cases went through at least eight steps in the forming process. Fulminate was then "spun" into the recesses of the rim, the powder charge was inserted, and a bullet was crimped in place. No headstamp.
Bullet: D .553, L .92, W 435   Cartridge: L 1.66

88 **.54 cal., Cosmopolitan** — Solid base, no grooves. A variant from St. Louis Arsenal features a punch-hole in the base. The linen cartridge case has paper pasted in place to close the bottom. This thin paper gave the percussion cap flame a place to penetrate the cartridge and ignite the powder charge.
Bullet: D .538, L .88, W 380   Cartridge: L 1.69

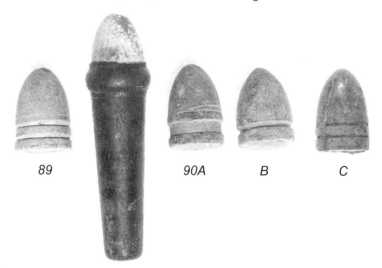

89   90A   B   C

89 **.54 cal., Burnside** — Two groove ball found with either a solid or dished base. The commonly recognized Burnside cartridge was made of drawn brass and features the "swell" around the bullet at the case mouth. This swell held lubricant and was patented by George P. Foster (#27,791 dated April 10, 1860). There is a variant of the cartridge, with a tinned case, that was assembled at the Frankford Arsenal.
Bullet: D .564, L .80, W 378   Cartridge: L 2.34

90 **.54 cal., Burnside** — Three variants. "A" is the "modified ball" approved in 1864 with one wide groove and a solid base. "B" has a pointy nose and a shallow cone cavity. "C" has a punchmark in the bottom and appears to be a machine-pressed variant.

Bullets: *A - D .557, L .81, W 389*   *B - D .554, L .76, W 332*
C - D .565, L .852, W 419

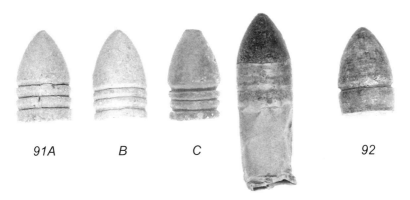

91A   *B*   *C*   *92*

91 **.54 cal., Merrill** — Solid base, three grooves. There are many variations to be found in the groove patterns of these bullets. The cartridge was made of paper and pasted to the bullet. Examples made with red cartridge paper also exist and are attributed to St. Louis Arsenal.

Bullets: *A - D .549, L .89, W 417*   *B - D .550, L .89, W 419*
C - D .540, L .892, W 383   *Cartridge: L 1.66*

92 **.54 caliber, Richmond Merrill** — Solid base, one groove, tapered base. A knife-cut is usually visible in the groove. This bullet was made at the Richmond Laboratory for captured or pre-Civil War Merrill carbines. See #35 and #59 for similarities.

Bullet: D .545, L .84, W 382

93

93   **.54 cal., Greene rifle** — Solid base, spherical nose. As found in European cartridges, the bullet faces toward the powder charge.
Bullet: D .545, L 1.00, W 571   Cartridge: L 2.01

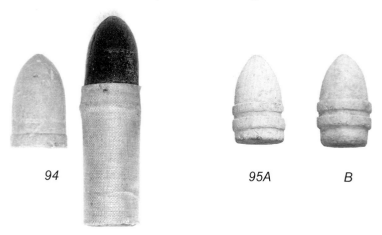

94   95A   B

94   **.54 cal., Starr** — These bullets feature one raised band around the base. This bullet has a solid base but variants exist with a machine punch-mark. The cartridge is of linen with plain paper pasted in place to close the end. Cartridge variants with blue paper used to seal the end are attributed to St. Louis Arsenal.
Bullet: D .552, L .91, W 443   Cartridge: L 2.00

95   **.54 cal.** — For an unknown breechloading carbine. The bullets have two raised bands and a solid, rebated base. "A" has been called a "Joslyn" for Spencer or Joslyn carbines but it does not appear to have been intended for a metallic cartridge. The recessed area around the base is more consistant with bullets that had paper, linen, or other combustible cartridges pasted to them. There is no evidence of the "crimp marks" from a metallic case like those found on Spencer bullets. "B" has a similar profile but with more pronounced features. This bullet is sometimes called a "Hall" by collectors.
Bullets: A - D .535, L .868, W   B - D .551, L .91, W 414

96   **.56 cal., Colt revolving rifle** — Solid with two grooves. Additionally, "A" has a slightly rebated base and was probably made by Colt. "B" which has a small punch-mark in the base was probably made by the Hazard Powder Co.
Bullets: A - D .568, L .96, W 475   B - D .570, L .96, W 484
Cartridges: A - L 1.82   B - L 1.74

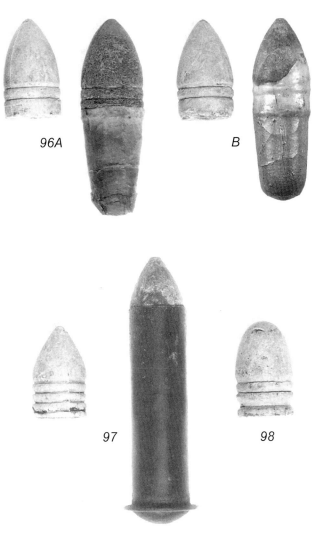

96A   B

97   98

97   **.52 cal., Billinghurst & Requa** — Solid bullet with four grooves. For the 25-barrel Billinghurst & Requa battery gun. The cartridge case cylinder was attached to a machined base containing the ignition hole.

     Bullet: D .545; L .88; W 381   *Cartridge: L 2.54*

98   **.58 cal., Lindner** — Solid base with three grooves. There is also a variant with a machine punch-hole. The Lindner carbine used a paper cartridge with a yarn "stopper" plugging the end.

     Bullet. D .575, L .92, W 511

SHARPS PISTOLS, CARBINES, RIFLES & SPORTING RIFLES, .36 TO .56 CALIBER

Originally Sharps rifles were classified by "bore size" instead of by "caliber." These early sporting rifles were available in 90, 60, and 32-bore. These measures translate into approximately .38, .44, and .52 caliber respectively.

Sharps weapons were breechloaders and used a solid bullet that was of a larger diameter than the bore. The raised bands easily grabbed the rifling of the gun barrel. The variety of small cavities found in the "new model" bullets were all created by bullet-machine punches.

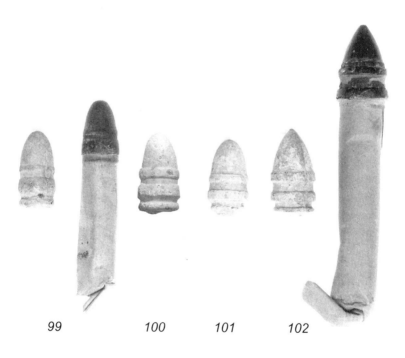

99   100   101   102

99   **.36 cal., Sharps** — For Sharps pistols manufactured between 1857-1858. Solid bullet, raised bands, tie ring, nipped sprue on base. This pattern of bullet, with extended ring, is known as a "ringtail." This ringtail, or tie ring, was where the cartridge case was tied to the bullet with string. The case was filled with powder and closed by the regulation folds which produced a tail.
Bullet: D .373, L .74, W 157   Cartridge: L 1.97

100 **.44 cal., Sharps** — For Sharps sporting rifle. Solid bullet, tie ring, nipped sprue on base. Civilian pattern with two bands.
Bullet: D .443, L .766, W 214

101 **.38 cal., Sharps** — For Sharps sporting rifle. Solid bullet, tie ring, nipped sprue on base. Civilian pattern with two bands.
Bullet: D .425, L .75, W 187

102 **.44 cal., Sharps** — For Sharps sporting rifle. Solid bullet, tie ring, nipped sprue on base. Civilian pattern with two bands. Paper cartridge tied to bullet with the end closed by folds.
Bullet: D .453, L .85, W 234   Cartridge: L 2.86

103   104   105   106

103 **.38 cal., Sharps** — Multi-grooved bullet, raised bands above and below grooves, tie ring, nipped sprue on base. This "multi-groove" bullet design was by Gomez and Mills who held U.S. patent #21,253, dated August 24, 1858.
Bullet: D .393, L .71, W 150

104 **.44 cal., Sharps** — Gomez and Mills multi-grooved bullet, raised bands above and below grooves, tie ring, nipped sprue on base.
Bullet: D .470, L .81, W 242

105 **.44 cal., Sharps** — Gomez and Mills multi-grooved bullet, variant with only one raised band, tie ring, nipped sprue on base. Cartridge case of plain untreated paper.
Bullet: D .492, L .88, W 289   Cartridge: L 2.76

106 **.52 cal., Sharps** — Gomez and Mills multi-grooved bullet, raised bands above and below grooves, tie ring. Cartridge case of plain untreated paper.
Bullet: D .562, L .99, W 455   Cartridge: L 2.38

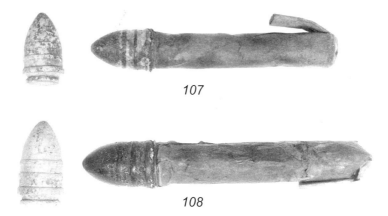

107

108

107 **.38 cal., Sharps** — For sporting rifle. Solid bullet, tie ring. Military pattern with three bands. Paper cartridge case.
Bullet: D .425, L .70, W 163   Cartridge: L 2.48

108 **.44 cal., Sharps** — For sporting rifle. Solid bullet, tie ring. Military pattern with three bands. Paper cartridge case.
Bullet: D .467, L .83, W 259   Cartridge: L 2.85

109 **.44 cal., Sharps** — For sporting rifle. "New model" bullet with solid base, three raised bands. Cartridge case made of Linen.
Bullet: D .486, L .82, W 259

110 **.52 cal., Sharps** — U.S. arsenal-made "new model" bullet. Two raised bands, rebated base. Machine-made punch mark in base. Paper cartridge case pasted to bullet.
Bullet: D .537, L .89, W 391   Cartridge: L 2.28

111 **.52 cal., Sharps** — Solid base, two raised bands. Possibly an early version of #112. Records indicate that Richmond initially made their Sharps bullets too small in diameter.
Bullet: D .525, L .98, W 424

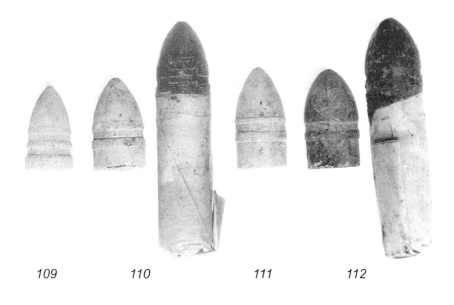

109   110   111   112

112 .52 cal., Richmond Sharps — Made at the Richmond Laboratory for Sharps carbines. Solid bullet, one groove, rebated base.
  Bullet: D .548, L .95, W 473 *Cartridge: L 2.26*

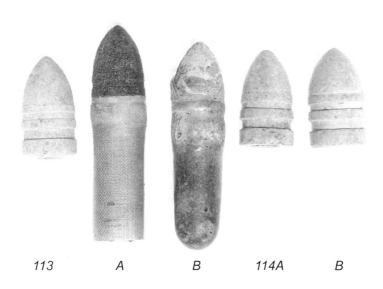

113   A   B   114A   B

113   **.52 cal., Sharps** — This is the bullet for the "new model" carbine and is probably the most common Sharps bullet. It has a solid base with a noticeable mark where the sprue was removed.
Bullet: D .538, L .99, W 444

Commonly encountered Sharps cartridges were made of linen and nitrated paper (made by Johnston & Dow).
Cartridges: ***A** - L 2.06*   ***B** - L 2.00*

114   **.52 cal., Sharps** — Two variants of the "new model" bullet. These machine-pressed bullets are found with a variety of cavities: small cone, truncated cone, and with teats of varying lengths.
Bullets: ***A** - D .535, L .93, W 401*   ***B** - D .538, L .95, W 425*

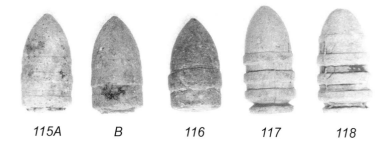

115A   *B*   *116*   *117*   *118*

115   **.52 cal., Sharps** — Two variants. Solid bases, layers of feintly defined raised bands.
Bullets: ***A** - D .538, L .98, W 440*   ***B** - D .540, L .97, W 443*

116   **.52 cal., Sharps** — Unusual variant with solid base and one wide band around the middle of the bullet. Unknown origin.
Bullet: D .560, L .92, W 424

117   **.52 cal., Sharps** — "Old model" pattern. Solid bullet, three raised bands, tie ring.
Bullet: D .538, L 1.08, W 465

118   **.52 cal., Sharps** — Similar to above with extra band below the nose. Called the "4-ring" Sharps by collectors.
Bullet: D .550, L 1.03, W 477

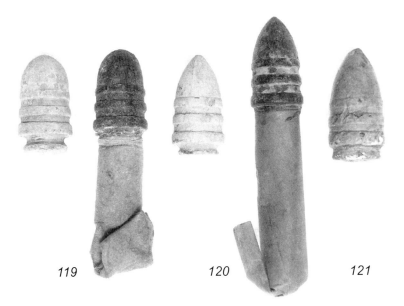

119   120   121

119   **.52 cal., Sharps** — Solid bullet, three raised bands, tie ring, round nose. Paper cartridge tied to bullet.
Bullet: D .556, L 1.00, W 464   Cartridge: L 2.30

120   **.52 cal., Sharps** — Solid bullet, three raised bands, tie ring, pointy nose. Paper cartridge tied to bullet with the end closed by folds.
Bullet: D .546, L 1.01, W 423   Cartridge: L 2.75

121   **.56 cal., Sharps** — Ringtail pattern with deep cavity (0.535 deep).
Bullet: D .569, L 1.12, W 471

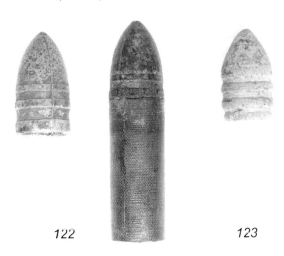

122   123

41

122 **.56 cal., Sharps** — Solid base. For the .56 caliber "New Model" 1859 rifle originally made for the Navy. Linen cartridge case.
Bullet: D .576, L 1.04, W 540   Cartridge: L 2.18

123 **.52 cal., Sharps** — Solid base, two grooves, possible tie ring. This unusual pattern is called the "Bavarian" Sharps but may not have even been for the Sharps. There is also a variant with a cone cavity.
Bullet: D .533, L .91, W 395

124   125   126

124 **.52 cal., Sharps & Hankins** — Bullet has three raised rings and a "pin" protruding from the base. The "pin" held a linen wad in place between the bullet and the powder charge. Copper rimfire cartridge, no headstamp, for Second Model Sharps & Hankins.
Bullet: D .53, L 1.115, W 438   Cartridge: L 1.77

125 **.52 cal., Sharps & Hankins** — Solid base with one wide groove. Self-contained rimfire cartridge for the First Model Sharps & Hankins. No headstamp. Until recently this round was mistakenly identified as being for the Ballard carbine.
Bullet: D .550, L .85, W 407   Cartridge: L 1.68

126 **.36 cal., Sharps** — Reloadable "mule ear" cartridge for Sharps lever action pistols made 1857-1858. A drawn brass case with an "ear" soldered to the base. The ear aided in extracting the case after firing. A hole in the base allowed the flame from the cap to ignite the powder charge.   *Cartridge: L 1.56*

RIFLES, RIFLE MUSKETS, AND SMOOTHBORE MUSKETS
.54 TO .73 CALIBER

The infantry weapons commonly used during the Civil War were the rifle musket and the smoothbore musket. Both of these were muzzleloaders (powder and bullet loaded from the muzzle and rammed down the barrel) and were fired using a percussion cap. One common characteristic of bullets for both smoothbores and rifle muskets was that they had to have a smaller diameter than the bore of the gun so they would fit down the barrel during loading. The space between the bullet and the barrel was called windage. During the Civil War, most of the bullets made in the North were machine pressed, which produced a more solid and uniform ball. The South, however, predominately cast their bullets in moulds. Often the only way to distingish between a Northern and Southern "3-groove minnie" is if it shows some "cast" features. These features include a noticable sprue location (nose cast, side cast, etc.) or irregularities in the cavity and/or rings.

The Smoothbore Musket

The smoothbore musket, as the name indicates, had a smooth bore in the barrel. The projectile generally employed was a spherical ball or round shot. Because of the windage in smoothbores the ball does not take a true or straight path as it travels through and exits from the barrel, but tends instead to bounce from side to side and take an erratic course when it leaves. Smoothbores were very inaccurate at ranges over 50 yards and were useless over 100 yards. Although inaccurate, the great demand by both governments for serviceable weapons meant that the outdated smoothbore saw service in great quantities throughout the war.

The Rifle Musket

The rifle musket (RM) was the standard infantry shoulder arm in use during the Civil War. It had a rifled barrel and used an elongated ball most commonly in .58 caliber. These bullets needed some feature that allowed them to expand into the rifling upon being fired – this feature was usually a cavity in the base. Another common characteristic was a number of rings around the body of the bullet. These rings held a lubricant of wax and tallow.

.54 caliber — Ammunition of this caliber was intended for the U.S. and M1841 "Mississippi" rifle, .54 and .55 caliber foreign rifle muskets (especially Austrian).

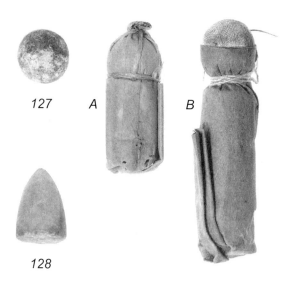

127   A   B

128

127   **.54 cal., round ball** — Solid round ball. "A" is the regulation paper pistol cartridge and "B" is a "patched" ball cartridge. A "patched" ball was a bullet that was wrapped in cloth in an attempt to eliminate the windage and have it take the rifling.
     Bullet: D .536, W 221   *Cartridge:* **A** *- L 1.49*   **B** *- L 2.38*

128   **.54 cal., Mississippi rifle** — Solid bullet, pointy nose, nipped sprue on base. This is the elongated ball for the Mississippi rifle cast in moulds fabricated before the war at Harpers Ferry. The Confederates continued to use these old moulds and refered to these bullets as "Harpers Ferry Slugs" in their production reports.
     Bullet: D .534, L .75, W 299

129   **.54 cal., RM** — Northern manufacture. Five variants of the common three-groove bullet with cone cavity. It should be remembered that the cartridges were handmade and that probably no two are exactly alike. Minor variations in paper, string, or length of the cartridge should be expected and not considered unusual.
     Bullets: **A** *- D .528, L 1.04, W 424*   **B** *- D .535, L 1.02, W 406*
               C *- D .533, L .94, W 368*   **D** *- D .536, L .97, W 397*
               E *- D .525, L .87, W 338*   *Cartridge: L 2.436*

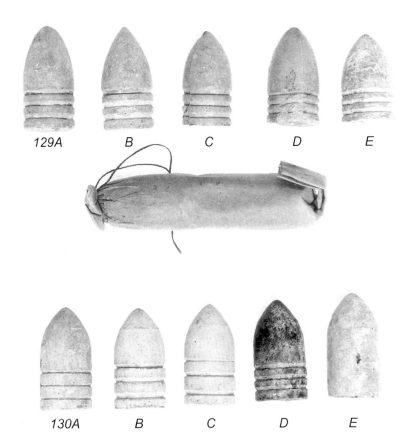

129A   B   C   D   E

130A   B   C   D   E

130 **.54 cal., RM** — Northern manufacture, machine made. All have a cone cavity, four have three grooves, while the fifth has none. Five variants, the differences are only in the rings. These were "pressed and turned" by machine. A slug was pressed by two punches to form the nose and cavity. It was then turned on a lathe to shape the body and cut the rings. See also #150, 188.

Bullets: *A* - D .538, L 1.02, W 448   *B* - D .538, L .99, W 433
          C - D .537, L 1.00, W 437   *D* - D .538, L 1.00, W 447
          E - D .537, L 1.04, W 457

131 **.54 cal., Gardner** — Frederick Gardner received a Confederate patent for this bullet and cartridge. See #162 and Appendix 2.

Bullet: D .536, L 1.08, W 441   *Cartridge: L 2.49*

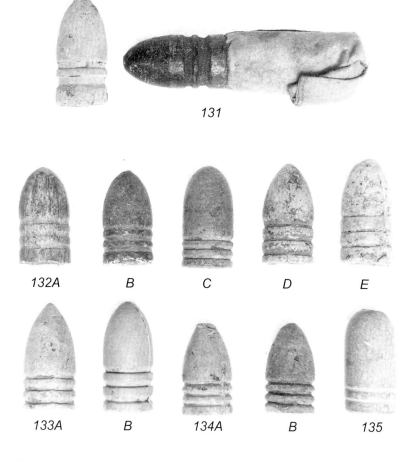

131

132A *B* *C* *D* *E*

133A *B* *134A* *B* *135*

132 **.54 cal., RM** — Southern manufacture. All have three grooves and a plug or truncated cone cavity. Five variants. "A,"wrongly termed a "salvaged lead" bullet by collectors, was a late-war product of Richmond and may be machine pressed. "B" through "E" were cast. "E" is attributed to the Selma Arsenal and can also be found with a cone cavity.

*Bullets: **A** - D .518, L .96, W 390* * **B** - D .530, L .94, W 401*
* **C** - D .538, L 1.01, W 431* * **D** - D .534, L 1.00, W 383*
* **E** - D .539, L 1.05, W 447*

133 **.54 cal., RM** — Southern manufacture. Three grooves, nose cast, cavity with a teat. Two variants.

*Bullets: **A** - D .535, L 1.06, W 417* * **B** - D .515, L 1.08, W 450*

134 **.54 cal., RM** — Southern manufacture. Three grooves, nose cast, with a dished base cavity. Two variants. The cavity in "A" is shallow (0.13 deep). "B" has a deeper cavity (0.22 deep).
Bullets: ***A*** *- D .525, L .91, W 354*   ***B*** *- D .517, L .89, W 342*

135 **.54 cal., RM** — Two grooves, nose cast, parabolic cavity. Can also be found with truncated cone and teat cavities. Probably made in Marshall, Texas.
Bullet: D .528, L 1.00, W 492

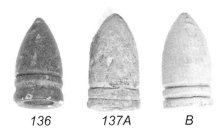

136   137A   B

136 **.54 cal., RM** — Two grooves, nose cast, elliptical cavity.
Bullet: D .530, L .90, W 295

137 **.54 cal., RM** — Two grooves, cone cavity. "B" is side cast. These may also have been intended for a "Tennessee rifle." (See #64).
Bullets: ***A*** *- D .535, L .96, W 405*   ***B*** *- D .530, L .97, W 392*

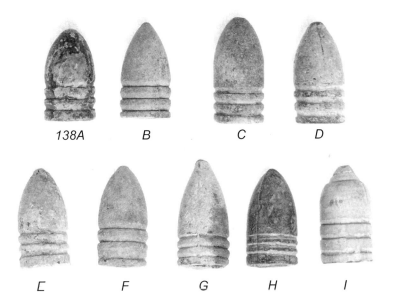

138A   B   C   D

E   F   G   H   I

138 **.54 cal., RM** — Southern manufacture. All of these have a cone cavity and were nose cast. Nine variants.

Bullets: *A* - D .535, L 0.91, W 402   *B* - D .532, L 0.95, W 368
      C - D .528, L 1.04, W 452   *D* - D .524, L 1.00, W 385
      E - D .526, L 0.98, W 392   *F* - D .530, L 1.00, W 405
      G - D .538, L 1.08, W 415   *H* - D .538, L 0.97, W 407
      I - D .534, L 0.97, W 423

   139   140   141A   B   142

139 **.54 cal., Charleston RM** — Nose cast with cone cavity. Known as the "high base" due to the distance from the base to the grooves. Made at the Charleston Arsenal. See also #169.
     Bullet: D .535, L 1.10, W 471

140 **.54 cal., RM** — Southern manufacture. Three faint grooves with elliptical cavity (.287 deep). Notice the vertical cut marks on the bullet. These came from slits made in the cartridge, a feature usually evident on Enfield cartridges.
     Bullet: D .520, L .88, W 378

141 **.50 and .54 cal., Wilkinson** — Solid base with two deep grooves. Following a European design, these were produced by the state of North Carolina for its troops armed with .50 and .54 caliber "North Carolina rifles." Upon firing, the two small wedge-shaped segments formed by the deep rings were compressed toward the nose of the bullet. This compression forced the thin edges of each segment into the rifling.
     Bullets: *A* - D .498, L .95, W 413   *B* - D .540, L .97, W 479

142 **.54 cal., RM** — Three raised rings, elliptical cavity. Often called an "Italian Carcano" or "Garibaldi" by collectors. Manufactured by the state of North Carolina.
     Bullet: D .537, L .97, W 324

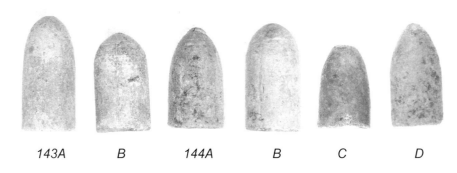

143A   B   144A   B   C   D

143 **.54 cal., RM** — Like Enfields, these have no grooves. These appear to be machine pressed. "A" has a cone cavity, "B" has a plug cavity with a raised dot in the center.

    Bullets: **A** - *D .519, L 1.12, W 511*   **B** - *D .525, L .96, W 422*

144 **.54 cal., RM** — Similar to #143 except that these were cast. All have cone cavities. "D" is a Marshall, Texas, Enfield (see also #148).

    Bullets: **A** - *D .537, L .92, W 401*   **B** - *D .518, L .98, W 450*
                 C - *D .520, L .82, W 315*   **D** - *D .525, L 1.01, W 415*

144.5

144.5 **.54 cal., RM** — Southern manufacture. The upper portion of this bullet is similar to #132E. This strange bullet appears to have been cast in a mould without a proper base plug. There is a hole in the extended base .18" diameter and .9" deep. Because of the hole, appearently for a stick, it has been suggested that this was for a southern version of the Von Lenk gun-cotton cartridge. However, there is no documented proof of this.

    Bullet: D .540, L 1.250, W 559

.577 caliber — Ammunition of this caliber was intended for the Enfield P-1853 rifle, but could also be used in the .58 caliber Springfield rifle musket. Enfield pattern bullets were not used by the Northern army. The Confederacy imported them through the blockade or cast them in imported or locally made moulds. The variations in height and base markings are so numerous that Enfields can grow into a collection of their own. For this reason the number has been intentionally limited here.

Enfield bullets made in England were machine pressed. A slug of lead was pressed into a die which formed the nose and cavity. The punch that formed the cavity was often engraved and left a number, letter, or symbol in the base of the bullet. These markings in the base may have been a way to check for worn punches. See Appendix 3 for cavity markings.

Two interesting features of the Enfield were the use of a boxwood plug to expand the bullet and the upside-down positioning of the bullet in the cartridge. In many European countries the cartridges were wrapped so that the nose of the bullet rested upon the powder charge. The lubricant was applied to the exterior of the cartridge; the waxed paper and bullet were intended to be loaded together.

English-made Enfield cartridges.
(Top to bottom) Typical English-made, unmarked white paper cartridge.
White paper with green label, "E. & A. Ludlow. Birmingham."
White paper with "Eley Bros London" impressed into the paper.

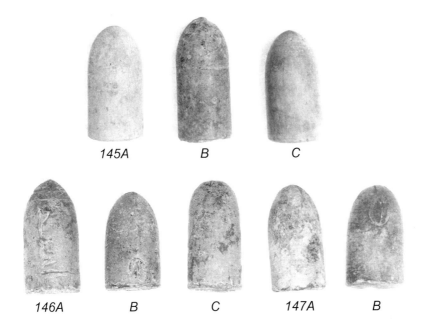

145A   B   C

146A   B   C   147A   B

145   **.577 cal., Enfield** — No grooves, plug cavity, machine pressed. "A" has a cavity with a raised dot, "B" has a plain plug cavity, and "C" has a plug cavity with a raised "57".

> *Bullets:* ***A*** *- D .567, L 1.08, W 588*   ***B*** *- D .550, L 1.18, W 563*
> ***C*** *- D .568, L 1.06, W 521*

146   **.577 cal., Enfield** — Cast with cone cavity. Three variations.

> *Bullets:* ***A*** *- D .570, L 1.13, W 610*   ***B*** *- D .569, L .97, W 516*
> ***C*** *- D .564, L 1.10, W 605*

147   **.577 cal., Enfield** — Cast. Two variations. Bullet "A" has a teat in the base, "B" was side cast – note where sprue was cut at the side of the nose.

> *Bullets:* ***A*** *- D .558, L 1.05, W 539*   ***B*** *- D .572, L 1.01, W 553*

148A   B

148   **.577 cal., Marshall Enfield** — Cast, cone cavity. Manufactured at the arsenal near Marshall, Texas. "B" is the rarer deep cavity.

> *Bullets:* ***A*** *- D .565, L .948, W 4/5*   ***B*** *- D .563, L .977, W 435*

.58 caliber — Ammunition of this caliber was used in the Springfield rifle musket and the .577 caliber Enfield rifle. Variations found in the grooves and profiles on these "minnies" is nearly infinite, so, like the Enfield specimens in the previous section, the number presented here has been intentionally limited.

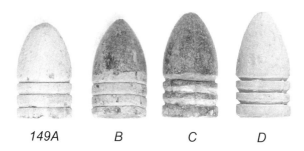

149A   B   C   D

149   .58 cal., Rifle Musket (RM) — This is the regulation 3-groove "minnie" with a cone cavity that was developed in the mid-1850s. Northern manufacture, four variations.

> *Bullets: A - D .568, L .95, W 466   B - D .570, L .98, W 438*
> *C - D .576, L 1.05, W 500   D - D .565, L 1.05, W 492*

Northern cartridges using the 3-groove minnie.
(L to R) The regulation cartridge; Johnston & Dow; Robert Chadwick; Bartholow Cartridge Co.

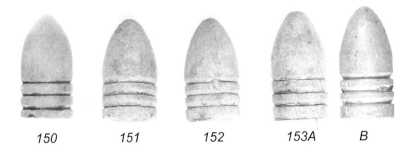

| 150 | 151 | 152 | 153A | B |

150 **.58 cal., RM** — Northern manufacture, pressed and turned, cone cavity. See also #130 and #188 for similarities.
Bullet: D .560, L 1.07, W 498

151 **.58 cal., RM** — Northern manufacture, with a star (☆) in the base. This bullet can be found with a small, medium, or large size star or a "five-lined" star in the base. The stars were formed by an engraved punch during the manufacturing process.
Bullet: D .571, L 1.00, W 478

152 **.58 cal., RM** — Northern manufacture, with "US" in the base. This "US," like the stars above, was formed by a punch during manufacturing.
Bullet: D .570, L 1.02, W 463

153 **.58 cal., RM** — Northern manufacture, pressed and turned with "spokes" in the base. These are often mistakenly referred to as "swaged" bullets. These were produced in machines made by J.D. Custer of Philadelphia. After a slug was pressed to form the nose and cavity, it was turned on a lathe to cut the three grooves. The spokes in the base were formed by the lathe chuck. "A" has six spokes, "B" has five spokes.
*Bullet: **A** - D .571, L 1.07, W 538   **B** - D .568, L 1.152, W*

Star in base,
base view.

US in base,
base view.

Pressed & Turned,
by Custer machine.

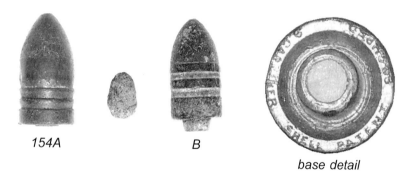

154A   B

base detail

154   .58 and .52 cal., Gardiner — Samuel Gardiner received patent #40,468 dated November 23, 1863 for his exploding bullet or "musket shell." These bullets have several distinctive characteristics. They have a dark color because they were cast of pewter which was harder than lead and would fragment. On good specimens, "S. Gardiner Jr. Shell Patent Secured" can be found in raised letters around the base. The fuse nozzle is easily found in the base of the .58 and protrudes from the base of the .54 bullet. The nozzle leads to a powder-filled copper vessel in the center of the bullet. The .52 explosive was patterned after the Sharps bullet, but it is not known whether these were intended for cavalry or sharpshooters.

*Bullets: **A** - D .570, L 1.12, W 372   **B** - D .538, L 1.12, W 339*

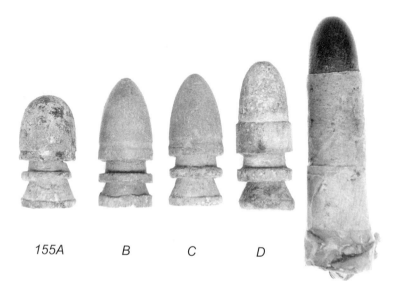

155A   B   C   D

155 **.58 cal., Shaler** — Ruben & Ira Shaler received patent #36,197 on August 12, 1862 for their sectional bullet. In theory, the pieces separated after exiting the barrel making "one man equal to three." However, the separate sections were inaccurate. The four common combinations are pictured. Three different nose pieces are shown. There are also three base pieces; solid, dished, and a shallow flat cavity. The cartridge's unique feature is a string "pull" in place of the usual tail.

Bullets: ***A*** *- D .575, L 1.07, W 517*   ***B*** *- D .577, L 1.27, W 605*
*   **C** - D .573, L 1.28, W 574*   ***D*** *- D .573, L 1.43, W 693*
Cartridge: L 2.63

.58 cal., Williams — Specimens #156 through #161 were manufactured by Elijah D. Williams. Williams' patent called for the use of zinc washers and a pin or plunger as a means for the bullet to take the rifling of the musket. In operation, the powder gases directly or indirectly flattened the washers causing them to expand into the rifling. The flattened washers also scraped away the fouling in the bore as they exited from the gun, hence the nickname "cleaners." The Williams bullet has a distinctive nose and rings. Cartridges made with Williams' bullets were made in the regulation manner, but they can be found in red, blue, white, and the usual tan paper.

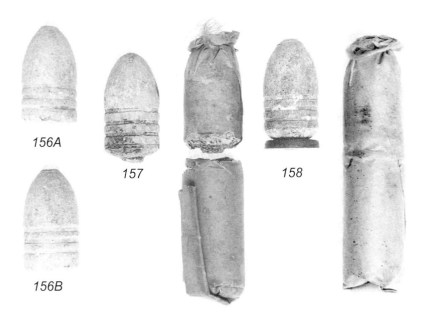

156A

156B

157

158

156 **.58 cal., Williams Regulation** — The typical Williams bullet with a regulation cone cavity, two variations.
Bullets: ***A*** *- D .563, L .94, W 458*   ***B*** *- D .566, L .98, W 481*

157 **.58 cal., Williams, Type I** — Patented May 13, 1862 (#35,273). Three rings with two zinc disks (with six slits in each) secured by a pin. Cartridges in tan and blue paper. Other than obtaining a broken (as pictured) or x-rayed specimen, the Williams regulation and type I cartridges are virtually indistinguishable from the standard .58 cartridge.
Bullet: D .574, L 1.09, W 546

158 **.58 cal., Williams, Type II** — Patented December 9,1862 (#37,145). Three rings with one disk (without slits) secured by a cast plunger. Cartridges in white or off-white paper.
Bullet: D .570, L 1.08, W 560   *Cartridge: L 2.49*

159 **.58 cal., Williams, Type III** — Two rings with one disk (no slits) secured by a cast plunger. Cartridges in red, blue, and tan paper.
Bullet: D .570, L .89, W 455   *Cartridge: L 2.43*

159   *160*   *161*

160 **.58 cal., Union repeating gun** — Early pattern with two deep "V" grooves, square pin and zinc washers. Made by Williams for use in the Union repeating gun (aka Coffee Mill gun, Agar). Cartridges were loaded into reuseable iron chambers. The chamber features a percussion cap nipple on the end. Although an excavated chamber is shown, the dimensions are from a non-dug specimen illustrating that this round will fit the chamber while being too large for the .58 rifle musket.

Bullet: D .578, L .93, W 450   Chamber: OD .959; L 2.97; ID .590

161 **.58 cal., Union repeating gun** — Later pattern with two square grooves and plunger to hold zinc washers. Made by Williams for use in the Union repeating gun (aka Coffee Mill gun, Agar).

Bullet: D .582, L 1.00, W 511

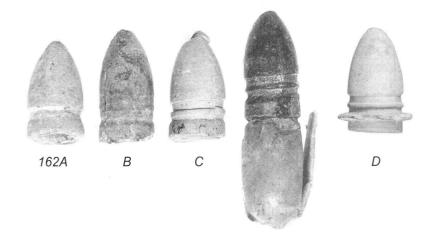

162A   B   C   D

162 **.58 cal., Gardner** — Two grooves, slotted skirt, three variations. These are nose cast bullets which account for many variations at the nose, depending on how the sprue was nipped. "A" is known as a "one ring" Gardner. "B" is often termed a "no ring" Gardner.

Frederick Gardner received Confederate patent #12 dated August 17, 1861, for his bullet and cartridge making machine. The bullet was cast with a flange around the bullet (see "D"). To make the cartridge, paper was rolled around a plunger to form the powder cylinder and a bullet was placed in a hole in the base plate. By using a foot peddle, the plunger (and paper cylinder) were lowered into the base of the bullet forcing it through the hole. In this one motion, the flange was crimped around the paper cylinder and the bullet was swaged to the proper diameter. The powder tube was then filled and its end folded in the usual manner. The majority of Gardner bullets were made at the Richmond Laboratory. Also see Appendix 2.

*Bullets: **A** - D .574, L .99, W 420   **B** - D .578, L 1.11, W 534*
*   **C** - D .578, L 1.10, W 490*
Cartridge: L 2.15

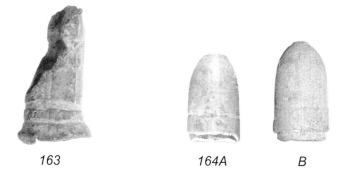

163   *164A*   *B*

163   **.58 cal., Gardner, "blow-through"** — Caused when an air bubble or some other flaw was cast into the bullet. Upon firing, the gases blew through the nose of the weak bullet.

164   **.58 cal., RM** — These have popularly been called "Tom Greene Enfields." Nose cast with truncated cone cavity, two variations in length. The bullet was cast with a perpendicular flange and the cartridge was made in the same manner as the Gardner. These were made at the Houston Ordnance Works and by the Dance & Parks company in Anderson, Texas.

*Bullets: **A** - D .568, L .86, W 416   **B** - D .576, L 1.026*

165   **.58 cal., RM** — Southern manufacture, nose cast with cone cavity. Four variations. These are basically the same as their northern counterparts, differing only in the way they were made.

*Bullets: **A** - D .572, L 1.03, W 489   **B** - D .568, L 1.07, W 525*
*   **C** - D .577, L .97, W 469   **D** - D .576, L .95, W 481*

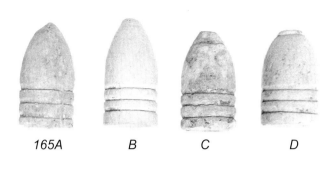

165A   B   C   D

166A

166B

166   **.58 cal., RM cartridges** — Southern manufacture for rifled muskets. "A" is from Macon Arsenal *(L 2.61)* and "B" is from Augusta Arsenal *(L 2.26)*.

167   **.58 cal., RM** — Nose cast, cone cavity. The "Spilman" pattern cartridge with the nose of the bullet left exposed was made at the Lynchburg Ordnance Depot, VA.
    Bullet: D .577, L 1.02, W 489   Cartridge: L 1.94

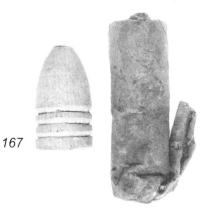

167

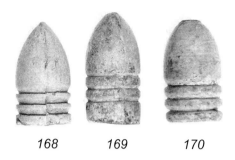

168   169   170

168 **.58 cal., RM** — Southern manufacture, side cast, cone cavity.
Bullet: D .574, L 1.02, W 488

169 **.58 cal., Charleston RM** — Southern manufacture, cone cavity, This is the "high-base" rifle musket ball made at the Charleston Arsenal. "High base" refers to the distance from the base to the grooves.
Bullet: D .561, L 1.12, W 545

170 **.58 cal., RM** — Southern manufacture, nose cast, round grooves, cone cavity. Variations in the depth of the cavity can be found.
Bullet: D .574, L 1.00, W 533

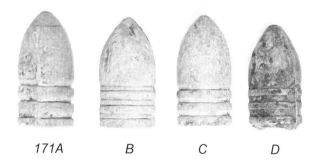

171A   B   C   D

171 **.58 cal., RM** — Southern manufacture, three grooves, teat in cavity, four variations.
Bullets: A - D .573, L 1.14, W 578   B - D .573, L 1.10, W 529
C - D .572, L 1.09, W 559   D - D .552, L 1.02, W 467

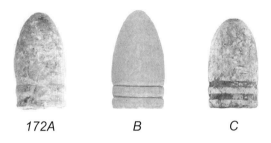

172A   B   C

172   **.58 cal., RM** — Southern manufacture, two grooves, cone cavity.
"C" has square grooves and its profile is similar to #194.

Bullets: ***A*** *- D .552, L 1.03, W 473*   ***B*** *- D .571, L 1.02, W 491*
C *- D .550, L .937, W 432*

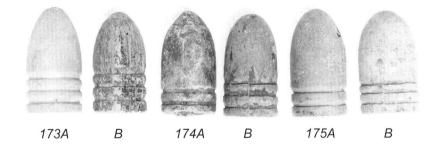

173A   B   174A   B   175A   B

173   **.58 cal., RM** — Southern manufacture, three grooves, plug cavity, two variations. "B" was made at Richmond. It is sometimes called a "salvaged lead" bullet due to its streaked exterior.

Bullets: ***A*** *- D .563, L 1.05, W 490*   ***B*** *- D .560, L 1.00, W 467*

174   **.58 cal., RM** — Southern manufacture, cone cavity, two and three groove variations.

Bullets: ***A*** *- D .575, L 1.03, W 516*   ***B*** *- D .565, L 1.02, W 518*

175   **.58 cal., RM** — Southern manufacture, plug cavity, two and three groove variations.

Bullets: ***A*** *- D .565, L 1.07, W 510*   ***B*** *- D .575, L 1.01, W 525*

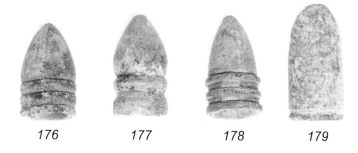

176   177   178   179

*Triangular-shaped
cavity, base view*

176 **.58 cal., French** — The French style with a triangular cavity. It was imported into the South from France. See also #195.
Bullet: D .570, L .95, W 378

177 **.58 cal., New Austrian** — Two deep grooves, solid base. Developed in Austria for the Lorenz rifle. Like the Wilkinson (#141), this bullet compressed when fired to "take" the rifling. Made in North Carolina.
Bullet: D .567, L 1.00, W 515

178 **.58 cal., RM** — Three raised bands, parabolic cavity. This is the scarcest of the three sizes. Produced by the state of North Carolina. Commonly called a "Carcano" or a "Garibali" by collectors.
Bullet: D .574, L 1.00, W 396

179 **.58 cal., RM** — Enfield-like bullet, one groove, teat base.
Bullet: D .560, L 1.15, W 572

.62 - .73 caliber — Ammunition in these calibers was intended for smoothbores, rifled conversions of smoothbores, foreign rifle muskets, and for shotguns.

180   *181A*   *B*

180   **.62 cal., Watervliet, RM** — For a French rifle. 485,000 of these were made into cartridges at the Watervliet Arsenal in 1861-62.
Bullet: D .616, L 1.00, W 497

181   **.63 cal., Charleston, RM** — No rings, shallow cone cavity. Two variations.   Made at the Charleston Arsenal for "two-groove" Brunswick rifles imported into the Confederacy.
*Bullet: **A** - D .618, L 1.00, W 593   **B** - D .628, L 1.04, W 672*

182   **.69 cal., Round ball** — For smoothbore muskets. "A" was cast "B" was machine pressed using a three-piece mould.
The round ball cartridges shown (L to R): pink paper with tan string made at the Augusta Arsenal *(L 1.96)*. Tan paper with red and white string *(L 1.77)*. Tan paper with brown string *(L 2.09)*.
*Bullets: **A** - D .648, W 408   **B** - D .650, W 409*

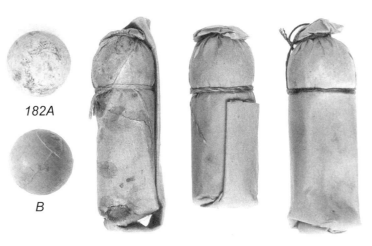

182A

B

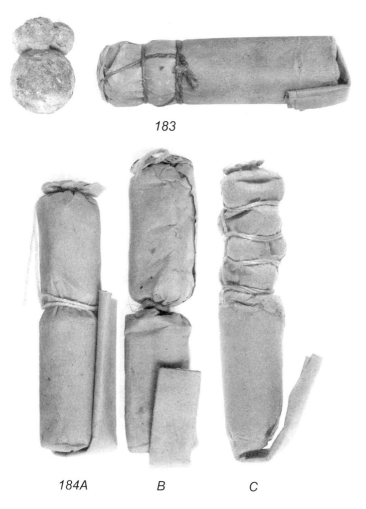

183

184A   B   C

183 **.69 cal., Buck & Ball** — Three .31 cal. buckshot packed with a .69 cal. round ball. This increased the chances of hitting a target when fired from the highly inaccurate smoothbore musket.
   Cartridge: L 2.47

184 **.69 cal., Buckshot** — Buckshot cartridges were made up of .31 caliber round shot for smoothbore muskets and shotguns. Cartridge "A" has twelve buckshot and was made at the Columbus (GA) Ordnance Depot *(L 2.62)*. "B" has fifteen buckshot and was made at Augusta Arsenal *(L 3.00)*. "C" is a regulation, Northern-made cartridge with half-hitches between each tier of shot.

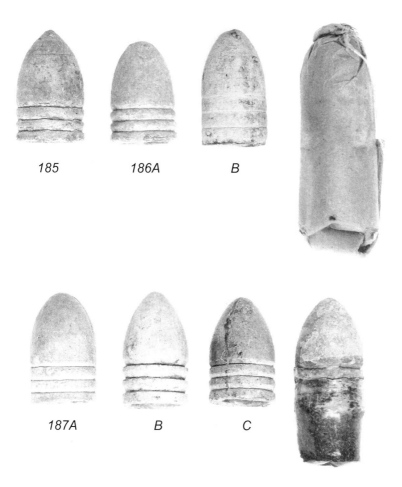

185   186A   B

187A   B   C

185   **.69 cal., Rifle Musketoon** — Three grooves, very deep plug cavity (.46 deep). Manufactured at the Frankford Arsenal in 1859.

> *Bullet: D .690, L 1.10, W 594*

186   **.69 cal., RM** — Three grooves, cone cavity. Two variations. The grooves on "B" are not very deep. The cartridge was made in the regulation manner *(L 2.23)*.

> *Bullets: **A** - D .680, L 1.01, W 678   **B** - D .676, L 1.15, W 766*

187   **.69 cal., RM** — Three grooves, cone cavity, typical Northern manufacture. Three variations. The cartridge was made by the Hazard Powder Company *(L 1.65)*.

> *Bullets: **A** - D .672, L 1.09, W 757   **B** - D .685, L 1.14, W 737*
> *   **C** - D .683, L 1.05, W 658*

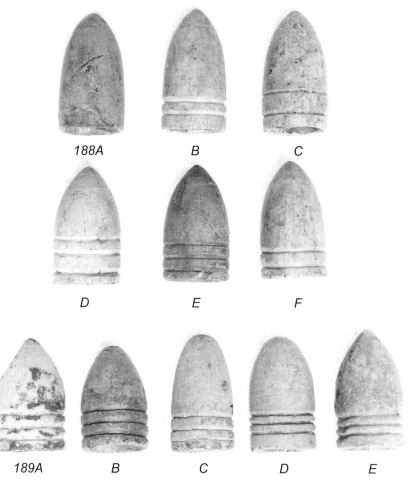

188A   B   C

D   E   F

189A   B   C   D   E

188   **.69 cal., RM** — Machine pressed and turned. Six variations, the differences are only in the rings. Northern manufacture. Misnamed "Prussians" by collectors. See #130 for similarities.

Bullets: ***A*** *- D .675, L 1.19, W 720*   ***B*** *- D .665, L 1.214, W 744*
         C *- D .670, L 1.21, W 742*   ***D*** *- D .685, L 1.16, W 768*
         E *- D .685, L 1.14, W 735*   ***F*** *- D .670, L 1.14, W 693*

189   **.69 cal., RM** — Five variations, cone cavities, typical Southern manufacture. "A" was side cast. "B" was nose cast. "E" was nose cast and is sometimes called a "Belgian" but it is doubtful that it was imported.

Bullets: ***A*** *- D .665, L 1.11, W 680*   ***B*** *- D .688, L 1.02, W 695*
         C *- D .664, L 1.16, W 711*   ***D*** *- D .676, L 1.13, W 803*
         E *- D .676, L 1.18, W 751*

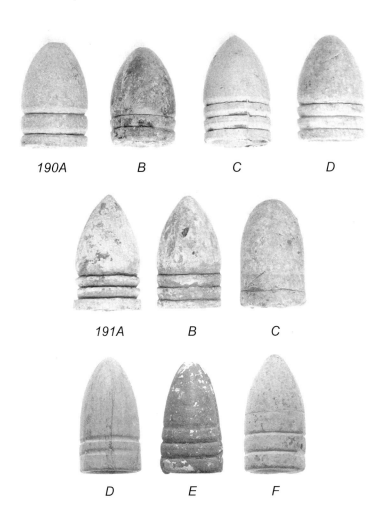

190A   B   C   D

191A   B   C

D   E   F

190   **.69 cal., RM** — Four variations. "A" has a cone cavity, and has been labeled a "Hessian." All the others have plug cavities.

Bullets: ***A*** *- D .680, L 1.04, W 724*   ***B*** *- D .685, L .97, W 564*
       C *- D .685, L 1.10, W 686*   ***D*** *- D .675, L 1.04, W 653*

191   **.69 cal., RM** — Four variations. "A" has an elliptical cavity, "B" has a solid base (probably cast without a base plug), "C" is an early ball with three faint rings and an iron cup in the cavity to aid in expansion, "D" has an ogival cavity and "E" is crudely cast. "F" has two grooves with a knife cut above them.

Bullets: ***A*** *- D .685, L 1.14, W 619*   ***B*** *- D .668, L 1.11, W 777*
       C *- D .675, L 1.06, W 644*   ***D*** *- D .675, L 1.225, W 754*
       E *- D .685, L 1.168, W 674*   ***F*** *- D .668, L 1.20, W 742*

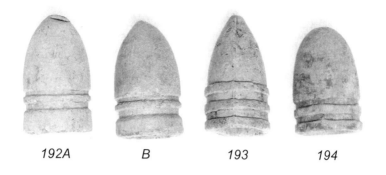

192A　　　　B　　　　193　　　　194

192 **.69 cal., Gardner** — This is the largest caliber of these bullets. "B" is the rarer type with a deep cavity (.438 deep).

Bullets: A - D .684, L 1.16, W 831   B - D .685, L 1.16, W 761

193 **.69 cal., RM** — This is the largest caliber of these "Carcanos." The 6th North Carolina is known to have used these bullets.

Bullet: D .667, L 1.17, W 616

194 **.69 cal., RM** — Two square grooves, cone cavity, nose cast. Associated with Louisiana troops. See #172C for similarities.

Bullet: D .675, L 1.03, W 721

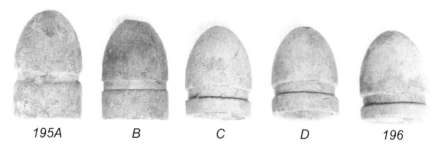

195A　　　　B　　　　C　　　　D　　　　196

195 **.69 cal., French** — French pattern with one groove, triangular cavity. Four examples. "A" is the crudest and rarest of these. "C" and "D" while having the same exterior profile, have different size triangular cavities.

Bullets: A - D .684, L 1.07, W 732   B - D .685, L .98, W 723
C - D .680, L .90, W 581   D - D .676, L .88, W 516

196 **.69 cal., French** — The French pattern with one groove. This variant has an elliptical cavity.

Bullet: D .677, L .89, W 503

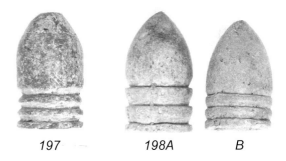

197   198A   B

197   **.69 cal., RM** — Three grooves, cone cavity, cast. This massive bullet has become known as an "Arkansas Hog." This is one of many rare bullet types to surface from the Trans-Mississippi.
Bullet: D .688, L 1.13, W 821

198   **.69 cal., RM** — Three grooves, teat base, cast. Southern manufacture. Two variations.
*Bullets: **A** - D .674, L 1.19, W 805   **B** - D .685, L 1.09, W 694*

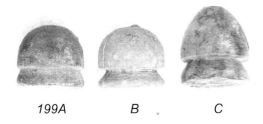

199A   B   C

199   **.69 cal., Nessler** — Solid ball, one groove, three variants. For use in smoothbore muskets, these so-called "shotgun slugs" were cast in Raleigh, N.C., for use by state troops. Copied from the Belgian Nessler pattern ball used during the Crimean War.
*Bullets: **A** - D .690, L .62, W 515   **B** - D .675, L .62, W 450*
*   **C** - D .680, L .77, W 558*

200   **.69 cal., British Rifled Musket** — No grooves, plug cavity, machine pressed. Two variants. For English P-51 rifled musket. Bullets of this pattern have commonly become known as "Tower" bullets to collectors.
*Bullets: **A** - D .664, L 1.14, W 838   **B** - D .675, L 1.03, W 758*

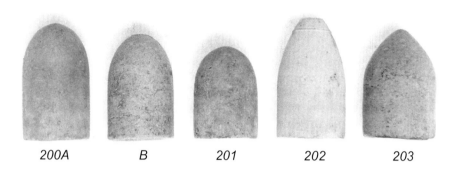

200A   B   201   202   203

201   **.69 cal., British RM** — No grooves, cone cavity, cast. These were made at several southern arsenals for British P-51 muskets and "Belgian rifles."
Bullet: D .667, L .90, W 600

202   **.69 cal., British RM** — No grooves, small plug cavity with raised dot, ring around nose. Unusual bullet shape. For P-51 rifle musket or "Belgian rifle."
Bullet: D .683, L 1.20, W 848

203   **.75 cal., British RM** — Pointy nose, cone cavity. For the older British P-42 rifled musket.
Bullet: D .718, L 1.06, W 751

204   **.69 cal., Explosive** — Southern manufacture. Believed to be a two piece explosive bullet. An iron nail or pin runs through the nose section and rested in a percussion compound at the base of the bottom section.
Bullet: D .688, L 1.15, W 679

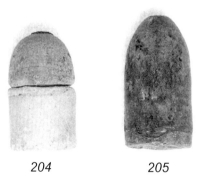

204   205

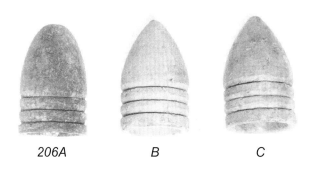

206A   *B*   *C*

205   **.69 cal., Explosive** — Southern manufacture. Believed to be another two piece explosive bullet, possibly made at the New Orleans Naval Laboratory.
Bullet: D .690, L 1.28, W 788

206   **.71 cal., RM** — For imported muskets. "A" and "B" have a cone cavity, "C" has a plug cavity.
Bullets: ***A*** *- D .698, L 1.08, W 765*   ***B*** *- D .700, L 1.13, W 717*
         C *- D .705, L 1.12, W 730*

207   **.72 cal., Round ball** — Cast, for use in the British P-42 smoothbore musket and the older "Brown Bess." The Confederacy is known to have produced cartridges for these at Nashville.
Bullet: D .702, W 497

208   **.72 cal., RM** — Three grooves, flat nose, very deep parabolic cavity. For imported muskets.
Bullet: D .714, L 1.06, W 707

209   **.72 cal., RM** — Three grooves, pointy nose, elliptical cavity.
Bullet: D .710, L 1.17, W 720

207   *208*   *209*

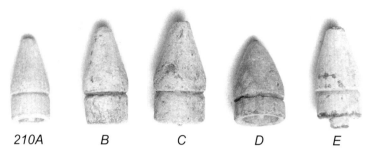

210A   B   C   D   E

210   **Dimick rifle bullets** — These are found in almost every diameter from .36 to .69 caliber. They feature numerous teat sizes and even cone cavities. Those shown above are just a sample.

These bullets are from moulds made by or for Horace E. Dimick of St. Louis, MO. The moulds were issued along with the Dimick American Deer and Target Rifles to "Birge's Western Sharpshooters" in 1861 and 1862. The Western Sharpshooters eventually became the 66th Illinois Infantry.

Bullets: ***A*** *- D .404, L .85, W 187*   ***B*** *- D .480, L .97, W 298*
           C *- D .545, L 1.03, W 411*   ***D*** *- D .530, L .85, W 303*
           E *- D .473, L 1.02, W 301*

211A   B   C   D   E

F

211   **Picket** — All have pointy noses and solid bases. These also are found in an endless variety. The cartridge case for "F" is of regular untreated paper glued to the ball *(L 1.36)*.

Bullets: ***A*** *- D .338, L .59, W 95*   ***B*** *- D .415, L .62, W 130*
           C *- D .400, L .71, W 148*   ***D*** *- D .453, L .77, W 221*
           E *- D .430, L .78, W 205*   ***F*** *- D .492, L .80, W 283*

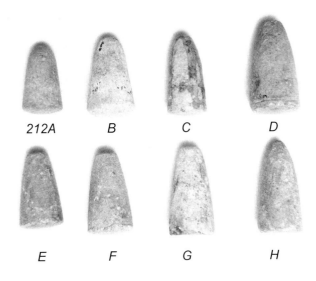

212A   B   C   D

E   F   G   H

212   Picket — Flat and round noses, solid bases. Eight variations. Bullets "C" and "D" have two faint rings.

Bullets: **A** - D .420, L .68, W 171   **B** - D .498, L .81, W 260
C - D .423, L .81, W 215   **D** - D .510, L .92, W 343
E - D .460, L .75, W 230   **F** - D .470, L .81, W 256
G - D .470, L .88, W 287   **H** - D .458, L .92, W 264

The "Picket" term pre-dates the Civil War and refers to all bullets of this conical nature. Pickets were used in the famed Kentucky or Pennsylvania rifles, as well as in some sharpshooting or target rifles.

GLOSSARY

Army and Navy Caliber Revolvers — The terms "Army" and "Navy," when associated with Civil War revolvers, can appear misleading. "Army" and "Navy" refer only to the caliber of an arm and in no way indicate its use by a particular branch of the armed forces. Army caliber revolvers are .44 caliber and Navy caliber revolvers are .36 cal. As nearly as can be determined, the terms originated with master salesman, Samuel Colt, in an attempt to enhance the sales of his arms to the two branches of the service.

Breechloading — The breechloading system allowed both projectile and gunpowder to be inserted into the arm through the breech or back end of the barrel. Breechloading significantly decreased loading time. This was a major advantage during the heat of battle.

Caliber — The inside diameter of a gun barrel stated in hundredths of an inch.

Carbine — The carbine is the shoulder arm of the cavalry. Because it was intended to be carried, and if necessary, used on horseback, the average length of the Civil War carbine was 39 inches. Loading a muzzleloading arm when on horseback is extremely difficult, if not almost impossible. For this reason most inventions of breechloading weapons were carbines. An inventor wishing to sell a new breechloading arm had a much better chance to do so if it was offered for cavalry use.

Collodion — A flammable liquid coating used on some cartridge cases to make them waterproof. Also frequently used as a means to reinforce the joint between the ball and the powder charge. Made by dissolving nitrated cellulose in a mixture of alcohol and ether.

Grain — A unit of measure. Bullet weights are in grains. There are 437.5 grains in an ounce.

Internal Primed Cartridges — These are totally self-contained cartridges. The bullet, powder, and primer are all in one sealed cartridge. Common examples are the rimfire, pin fire, cup fire, teat fire, and lip fire.

Musket — A musket is a smoothbore shoulder arm which fires a round lead ball. Smoothbore arms were standard issue in the U.S. Army until 1855, when they were replaced by a new model arm with a rifled bore. Although obsolete by the Civil War, many muskets were still in arsenal storage or in the hands of state militia units. In 1861, the average musket was 57 inches long and weighed about 9 pounds.

Muzzleloading — The muzzleloading system requires both the gunpowder and projectile to be inserted into the arm through the muzzle or front end of the barrel. Muzzleloading weapons were the standard issue to soldiers worldwide prior to and during the American Civil War.

Percussion Arms — Percussion means "striking" in music as well as in weaponry. Civil War small arms commonly used a small brass "cap" which contained a small amount of fulminate of mercury, a very volatile substance, to ignite the gunpowder charge which fired the weapon. A cap was placed on a cone or "nipple" that was mounted on the firearm in an area directly adjacent to the chamber. When loaded, the chamber contained the charge of black gun powder necessary to fire the bullet. The cap was the striking point of the firearm's hammer. The resulting percussion of the hammer strike caused the fulminate to explode, sending a tiny flame through a hole in the cone and into the powder charge. About 100 of these caps could be carried in a small leather pouch attached to a soldier's belt. Each bullet fired required a new cap.

Pistol — A pistol is a hand-held firearm. At the time of the Civil War most pistols were revolvers, however, a few single-shot muzzleloading varieties remained in use.

Pressed and Turned — A method of manufacturing bullets in the North. A machine pressed a lead slug to form the nose and cavity. This piece was then turned on a lathe to shape the body and cut the rings.

Revolver — A revolver is a hand-held firearm which includes a cylinder with a number of chambers (usually 6) containing cartridges. The cartridges were fired one at a time. During the Civil War, revolvers were issued primarily to cavalrymen, although some light artillerymen also carried them. Because of its convenient size and weight, the revolver was the weapon preferred by most officers.

Rifle — The rifle is a shoulder arm with a rifled bore. In the mid-19th century, the rifle was distinguished from the musket or rifle-musket by its length, which was usually about 49 inches. The shorter length of the rifle was ideal for mounted infantry troops or troops serving as skirmishers, where added maneuverability was important. When breechloading infantry arms were introduced at the time of the Civil War, the length of the rifle was considered to be perfect. These breechloading rifles also offered increased loading speed.

Rifling — In firearms this consists of cutting an evenly spaced number of spiral grooves in the inner surface of the barrel (bore). These grooves caused a projectile passing through the barrel to spin on its axis, thereby greatly increasing its accuracy. The United States Regular Army was not totally equipped with rifled small arms until after 1855.

Rifle-Musket — The rifle-musket is a shoulder arm with a length of about 56 inches which was manufactured with a rifled bore. The United States adopted its first rifle-musket in 1855. It quickly replaced the common musket as standard issue to the Regular Army. The model 1855 rifle-musket fired a new bullet shaped projectile known as the Minie ball. Its high degree of accuracy was a factor in the Civil War.

Rifled Musket — The rifled musket is a rifled shoulder arm which was originally manufactured with a smooth bore. When small arms with rifled bores became general issue in the U. S. Army after 1855, small arms with smooth bores became obsolete. As an economy measure, many of the stockpiles of smoothbore muskets on hand were sent back to various manufacturing points to have rifling grooves cut into the bore. These rifled muskets were issued to militia units or placed in storage for an emergency.

Separate Primed Cartridges — These are cartridges that are made up of ball and powder only. They need an outside (separate) source of ignition. Separate primed cartridges of non-combustible materials (rubber, foil, brass) all have a hole in the base to admit the percussion cap flame.

Smoothbore Arms — Smoothbore arms are those in which the inner surface of the barrel (bore) is entirely smooth. These arms fired a round lead ball which was cast slightly smaller than the diameter of the bore. This allowed the ball to be rammed down the barrel in preparation for firing. The ball would rest on the gunpowder charge which, when ignited, forced the ball out of the barrel. Smoothbore arms were used by the U. S. Army from the Revolution through the Civil War. The greatly increased accuracy of arms with rifled bores made smoothbore arms obsolete.

Swaged — A sizing process used on cast bullets. A bullet was placed in a metal cylinder of the desired shape and diameter. A punch the shape of the cavity followed and was struck with a hammer. This action swaged the bullet to proper diameter and shape. The bullet was dislodged by hitting a punch at the nose of the bullet.

Windage — The space between a projectile and the gun barrel. This space was essential in muzzleloading weapons to get the projectile down the barrel. However, this space had to be eliminated in order for the projectile to engage the rifling within the barrel when fired.

APPENDIX 1

Below are examples of the commonly encountered bullet characteristics referenced when describing bullet specimens.

CAVITIES

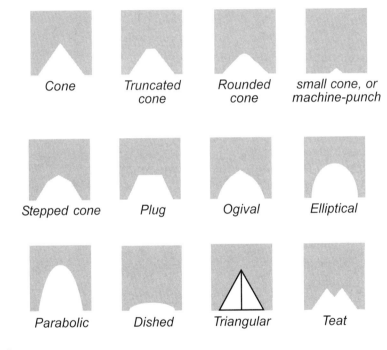

| Cone | Truncated cone | Rounded cone | small cone, or machine-punch |

| Stepped cone | Plug | Ogival | Elliptical |

| Parabolic | Dished | Triangular | Teat |

GROOVES

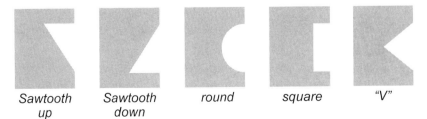

| Sawtooth up | Sawtooth down | round | square | "V" |

APPENDIX 2

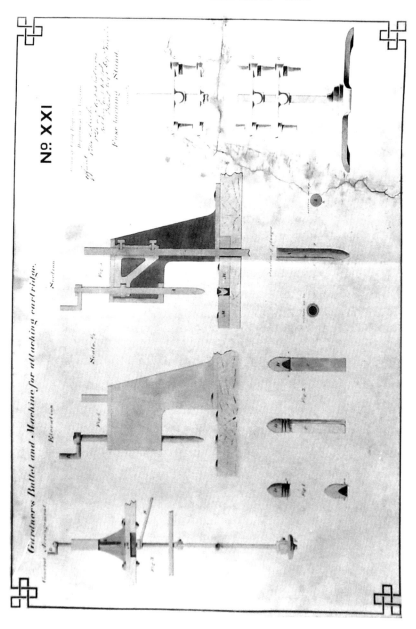

Plate No. XXI. Gardners method of attaching the paper cartridge to the Ball.

The object of this device was to expedite the manufacture of musket cartridges by superseding the necessity of tying the paper to the ball and at the same time swedge the ball to exact caliber and render the connection between it and the paper more accurate.

It is the invention of F.J. Gardner of N.C. and was used in the rebel arsenal at Richmond. The bullets were cast in the form shown in Fig. 1, having a circular flange, a, running around them immediately below the cannelures.

The paper was attached by turning down this flange upon the base of the ball, c, the paper, g, being caught between them as shown at, e, in Fig. 2. This was accomplished in a very simple manner in the machine shown in Fig. 3, 4, and 5.

The edge of the cartridge paper cut to proper size was inserted in the slot, b, of the steel plunger, A, and wound smoothly upon it by turning the handle, B.

The foot was then placed on the treadle, T, and the plunger and paper brought down on the bullet, D, forcing the latter through the swedging plate, M, the flange turned down and the paper caught.

Upon removing the foot from the treadle, the spring, S, lifts the plunger and the machine is ready to repeat the operation.

Lt. Michie's drawing No. XXI of "Gardner's Bullet and Machine for attaching cartridges" also included a sketch of a "Fuse burning Stand."

APPENDIX 3

Below are illustrations of the raised markings found in the cavities of the .577 caliber Enfield bullets that were manufactured in England and believed to be used in this country during the Civil War. These bullets were pressed on the "Anderson" bullet machine and the raised markings were created by an engraved punch during the process. It is believed that these markings helped inspectors check for worn forming punches, and also identified the machine on which they were made.

The "P" and "q" (reversed P) are believed to have been made by William Pursall. The "S" may have been made by Schlesinger & Wells' Ammunition Works in Kent. The "L", "L¹" and "L²" were manufactured by E. & A. Ludlow of Birmingham. The bullets numbered "1" through "8" were made at the Woolwich Arsenal and, being British government property, are the only specimens which exhibit the four "broad arrows" on the skirt around the base. The bullets with numbers "55" and "57" were made by Eley Brothers of London.

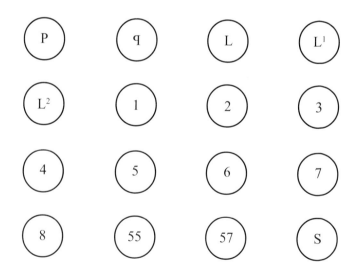

BIBLIOGRAPHY

Coates, Earl J. and Dean S. Thomas, *An Introduction to Civil War Small Arms*. Gettysburg, PA: Thomas Publications, 1990.

____. *The Field Manual for Use of the Officers on Ordnance Duty*. Richmond, 1862. Reprint. Gettysburg, PA: Thomas Publications, 1984.

Hoyem, George A. *The History and Development of Small Arms Ammunition, Volume One*. Tacoma, WA: Armory Publications, 1981.

Lewis, Berkeley R. *Small Arms and Ammunition in the United States Service, 1776-1865*. Washington, D.C.: Smithsonian Institution, 1956.

Logan, Herschel C. *Cartridges: A Pictorial Digest of Small Arms Ammunition*. New York: Bonanza Books, 1948.

McKee, W. Reid and M.E. Mason, Jr. *Civil War Projectiles II, Small Arms & Field Artillery*. Richmond, VA: Moss Publications, 1975.

Phillips, Stanley S. *Bullets Used in the Civil War, 1861-1865*. Lanham, MD: Stanley S. Phillips, 1971.

____. *Reports of Experiments with Small Arms for the Military Service by Officers of the Ordnance Department, U.S. Army*. Washington, D.C., 1856. Reprint. Arendtsville, PA: Dean S. Thomas, 1984.

Smith, Gene P. and Chris C. Curtis. *The Pinfire System*. San Francisco, CA: Bushman-Brashaw Pub. Co., 1983.

____. *Specifications and Drawings of Cartridges for Small Arms Patented in the United States prior to January 1, 1878*. Washington, 1878. Reprint. Tacoma, WA: Armory Publications, 1986

Suydam, Charles R. *U.S. Cartridges and Their Handguns, 1795-1975*. North Hollywood, CA: Beinfield Pub. Inc., 1977.

Thomas, Dean S. *Ready...Aim...Fire! Small Arms Ammunition in the Battle of Gettysburg*. Gettysburg, PA: Thomas Publications, 1993.

Round Ball to Rimfire: A History of Civil War Small Arms Ammunition. Parts One, Two, Three and Four. Gettysburg, PA: Thomas Publications, 1997, 2002, 2003.

CROSS-REFERENCE

The following list cross-references the specimens in this book (T&T) with those found in *Civil War Projectiles II* by McKee & Mason (M&M).

It was never the intended scope of this handbook to include all known bullets; only those that are commonly encountered or of special interest. Therefore, fired, carved, reproduction, and post Civil War bullets found in M&M will have no corresponding examples in this volume. Likewise, in the case of certain bullet patterns (i.e., Enfields, 3-ringers, Dimicks, Picket bullets, etc.) where M&M has liberally illustrated the numerous minor variations found, we chose to show only representative specimens here in T&T.

In the cartridge section of M&M where bullets are shown next to cartridges, please understand that in many cases these are only the *type* of bullet that *could possibly* be in that cartridge.

The following codes are used in this cross-reference:

–	=	Not listed in T&T
F/C	=	Fired or carved – not in T&T.
N	=	Not a Civil War era item – post-war, not known to be used, or may be a reproduction or souvenir – not in T&T.
-V	=	A variation of the bullet or cartridge noted.

M&M	T&T	M&M	T&T	M&M	T&T	M&M	T&T
Bullets		19	212f	39	N	59	212d
		20	212e	40	N	60	212-V
1	N	21	211-V	41	N	61	212c
2	211-V	22	211-V	42	122	62	212-V
3	211-V	23	211c	43	113	63	–
4	88	24	211-V	44	113-V	64	199a
5	88-V	25	211-V	45	F/C	65	199c
6	F/C	26	F/C	46	–	66	199b
7	88	27	211-V	47	N	67	92
8	211-V	28	211-V	48	109	68	–
9	F/C	29	211-V	49	72	69	F/C
10	F/C	30	211-V	50	72-V	70	73
11	128	31	211-V	51	100	71	90a
12	F/C	32	211-V	52	99	72	125
13	F/C	33	211-V	53	94	73	F/C
14	F/C	34	211-V	54	43a	74	78-V
15	F/C	35	211-V	55	43a	75	78
16	211-V	36	211-V	56	212-V	76	78-V
17	211-V	37	8	57	212-V	77	78-V
18	212g	38	N	58	212-V	78	–

M&M	T&T	M&M	T&T	M&M	T&T	M&M	T&T
79	F/C	131	36b	183	120	235	146-V
80	58	132	F/C	184	119-V	236	145-V
81	59	133	–	185	115a	237	F/C
82	32	134	37	186	117-V	238	146-V
83	32-V	135	87	187	117-V	239	–
84	77	136	91-V	188	117-V	240	146-V
85	38b	137	91-V	189	120	241	146-V
86	77-V	138	91a	190	120	242	146-V
87	5-V	139	91b	191	106	243	146-V
88	210-V	140	91-V	192	105	244	144a
89	35	141	96b	193	104	245	144a
90	21a	142	F/C	194	108	246	145-V
91	24a	143	98	195	102	247	148
92	24b	144	–	196	107	248	–
93	24b	145	97	197	101	249	–
94	25	146	13	198	101	250	65
95	25-V	147	91a	199	193	251	N
96	21a	148	96-V	200	178	252	N
97	19	149	N	201	142	253	F/C
98	–	150	16	202	94	254	F/C
99	38a	151	–	203	114b-V	255	211-V
100	39	152	–	204	114b-V	256	211-V
101	28	153	212-V	205	114b-V	257	211-V
102	–	154	212-V	206	114b-V	258	211-V
103	N	155	211-V	207	114a-V	259	211-V
104	–	156	212c	208	202	260	211-V
105	141a	157	212-V	209	–	261	N
106	141b	158	–	210	F/C	262	F/C
107	141b	159	68	211	188a	263	196
108	177	160	–	212	–	264	195d
109	177	161	F/C	213	201	265	195c
110	141a	162	F/C	214	200b-V	266	195b
111	70a	163	211-V	215	200a	267	195a
112	96b	164	17	216	181-V	268	179
113	F/C	165	5-V	217	201-V	269	80
114	87-V	166	55-V	218	F/C	270	80
115	113-V	167	55	219	–	271	F/C
116	96a	168	192b	220	143-V	272	F/C
117	96b	169	131	221	145b	273	90b
118	84	170	162c-V	222	144-V	274	F/C
119	89	171	162c-V	223	146-V	275	F/C
120	N	172	162c-V	224	146-V	276	210c-V
121	37	173	162c-V	225	146-V	277	210b-V
122	32	174	162c-V	226	145-V	278	210a-V
123	46	175	131	227	146-V	279	210-V
124	37	176	162b	228	145-V	280	210-V
125	27b	177	F/C	229	146-V	281	210-V
126	27a	178	118	230	146-V	282	210-V
127	36b	179	119	231	146-V	283	–
128	18	180	117-V	232	146-V	284	188b-V
129	F/C	181	F/C	233	F/C	285	188b
130	36b	182	117	234	145-V	286	188f

M&M	T&T	M&M	T&T	M&M	T&T	M&M	T&T
287	188c	339	188e	391	171c-V	443	75-V
288	188c	340	190d	392	171c-V	444	F/C
289	188f-V	341	173a	393	149-V	445	187a
290	191e	342	173a	394	149-V	446	189b
291	194	343	153	395	149-V	447	189b
292	190b	344	153	396	149-V	448	198a
293	190b	345	153	397	149-V	449	171b
294	N	346	153	398	149-V	450	165-V
295	F/C	347	153b	399	149-V	451	149-V
296	172	348	153	400	149-V	452	–
297	174s	349	176	401	149-V	453	138g
298	137b	350	175b	402	–	454	138-V
299	137b	351	149	403	165-V	455	129-V
300	F/C	352	156b	404	165d	456	149-V
301	135	353	156a	405	149-V	457	149-V
302	64c	354	153.5	406	F/C	458	149-V
303	64c	355	153.5	407	–	459	129-V
304	F/C	356	F/C	408	F/C	460	129-V
305	70c	357	F/C	409	173a	461	F/C
306	–	358	F/C	410	130d	462	111
307	F/C	359	F/C	411	129a	463	111
308	F/C	360	F/C	412	133a	464	112
309	89	361	F/C	413	133b	465	112
310	90c	362	F/C	414	176	466	111
311	85	363	149	415	138a	467	110
312	85	364	149	416	139	468	87
313	206b	365	165	417	133a-V	469	–
314	206c	366	169	418	132e	470	95a
315	206c	367	169	419	132e-V	471	87
316	189b	368	169	420	138-V	472	F/C
317	189b	369	149-V	421	138-V	473	F/C
318	189e	370	149-V	422	F/C	474	60a
319	189e	371	173b	423	N	475	116
320	198a	372	149-V	424	138a	476	144.5
321	198a	373	–	425	138e	477	F/C
322	–	374	–	426	138a	478	N
323	208	375	170	427	134a	479	58
324	189b	376	165a	428	138d	480	32
325	187b	377	165b	429	129c	481	61
326	187b	378	165b-V	430	132a	482	47
327	189b	379	168	431	129-V	483	62
328	186a	380	165-V	432	134b	484	N
329	185	381	165c-V	433	129-V	485	40
330	189a	382	–	434	129-V	486	61
331	189a	383	165c-V	435	132d	487	–
332	206a	384	149-V	436	132d	488	10
333	190c	385	149-V	437	129-V	489	10
334	187a	386	149-V	438	133a	490	10b
335	206c	387	149-V	439	63a	491	9
336	186b	388	149-V	440	129-V	492	9
337	188d-V	389	129-V	441	F/C	493	–
338	187b	390	171c	442	75	494	–

M&M	T&T	M&M	T&T	M&M	T&T	M&M	T&T
495	28	547	183	595	149-V	647	138-V
496	28	548	–	596	–	648	–
497	20	549	56	597	138h	649	F/C
498	28	550	183	598	165-V	650	–
499	7a	551	183	599	129-V	651	F/C
500	38b	552	F/C	600	149-V	652	12
501	–	553	–	601	149-V	653	F/C
502	51b	554	–	602	129-V	654	–
503	5-V	555	54a	603	169	655	121
504	51b	556	182	604	132a	656	F/C
505	5	557	–	605	165-V	657	164
506	6	558	–	606	138-V	658	22-V
507	4			607	168		
508	6	*Bullets in the*		608	190c-V	*Cartridges*	
509	3	*Supplement*		609	–		
510	N			610	N	1	186
511	210-V	559	190a	611	203	2	186
512	210-V	560	190b-V	612	210-V	3	166
513	N	561	188b	613	193	4	150a
514	160	562	188c	614	–	5	129
515	124	563	188f	615	211c	6	129
516	157	564	188d	616	211d	7	150a
517	23-V	565	189e	617	211e-V	8	150a
518	23b	566	190c	618	211-V	9	183
519	155a	567	206c	619	F/C	10	183
520	155b	568	187c	620	73	11	–
521	155d	569	206b	621	F/C	12	182b
522	155d-V	570	189e	622	123	13	182b
523	155c	571	198b	623	113	14	N
524	F/C	572	190d-V	624	F/C	15	162c
525	F/C	573	190c.	625	99	16	162c
526	–	574	F/C	626	F/C	17	–
527	–	575	187a	627	211b-V	18	120
528	–	576	187b	628	211b	19	–
529	N	577	190c	629	80	20	150b
530	205	578	187-V	630	–	21	91b
531	205	579	170	631	78	22	113c
532	154a	580	175b-V	632	32	23	129
533	204	581	175b	633	57	24	129
534	204	582	153.5	634	21a	25	N
535	N	583	171a-V	635	212b	26	159
536	–	584	132a	636	210	27	159
537	157	585	165-V	637	117	28	150a
538	158	586	173-V	638	10b	29	150a
539	161	587	173-V	639	10	30	166
540	159	588	165-V	640	95b	31	166
541	F/C	589	165-V	641	–	32	150a
542	160	590	156b	642	–	33	N
543	–	591	149-V	643	188a	34	–
544	F/C	592	129-V	644	172	35	69b
545	F/C	593	149c	645	172-c	36	N
546	F/C	594	129 V	646	188d-V	37	69c

M&M	T&T	M&M	T&T	M&M	T&T	M&M	T&T
38	144	90	23	142	15	196	91b
39	145a	91	23	143	15	197	38
40	145a	92	–	144	15	198	–
41	102	93	1b	145	15	199	–
42	102	94	44	146	15	200	150a
43	33b	95	44	147	131	201	150a
44	99	96	52a	148	112	202	150b
45	–	97	52a	151	15	203	150a
46	127	98	–	152	15	204	186
47	–	99	50c	153	51b	205	159
48	47	100	50a	154	–	206	129
49	–	101	–	155	13	207	7c
50	84	102	13	156	–	208	–
51	–	103	–	157	–	209	183
52	–	104	–	158	2	210	–
53	107	105	61	159	50c	211	113b
54	33a	106	51d	160	–	212	–
55	28	107	51c	161	60	213	183
56	28	108	51c	162	62	214	145b
57	5	109	51b	163	53	215	145
58	94	110	51a	164	87	216	145
59	20	111	53-V	165	87	217	145
60	113a	112	53-V	166	–	218	145
61	24a	113	53b	167	87	219	21
62	120	114	53b	168	80	220	21b
63	24a	115	53-V	169	78		
64	4	116	53a	170	77		
65	5	117	53-V	171	89		
66	36	118	124	172	124		
67	12-V	119	124	173	161		
68	40	120	124	174	97		
69	N	121	N	175	75		
70	N	122	125	176	125		
71	N	123	–	177	N		
72	N	124	87	178	126		
73	N	125	87	179	150b		
74	–	126	N	180	150b		
75	N	127	N	181	150b		
76	32	128	N	182	150b		
77	74a	129	N	183	72		
78	N	130	N	184	–		
79	72	131	N	185	150b		
80	N	132	97	186	150b		
81	81	133	161	187	150b		
82	74b	134	N	188	113c		
83	76a	135	–	189	51c		
84	76a	136	N	190	10		
85	89	137	128	191	45		
86	80-V	138	–	192	–		
87	77	139	–	193	40		
88	80	140	–	194	–		
89	23	141	15	195	60		

Cartridges were packaged in wrappers and boxes. Below are three examples of these wrappers. Like bullets and cartridges, an entire collection can be built solely from the variety of wrappers available.

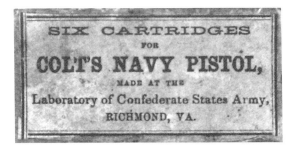

ABOUT THE AUTHORS

James E. Thomas, born and raised in southern New Jersey, and a 1985 graduate of Rutgers University, has studied the American Civil War for many years. An avid collector of Civil War, World War I and World War II relics and other military memorabilia, he is production manager for Thomas Publications in Gettysburg, Pennsylvania. He resides in Biglerville, Pennsylvania, with his wife, Ellen, and four children, James, Sarah, Zachary and Catherine.

Dean S. Thomas, born and raised in southern New Jersey, first visited Gettysburg in 1960. Interest in the Civil War and the collecting of Civil War artifacts began with the start of the Centennial celebration the following year. During college, he spent five summer seasons as a Licensed Battlefield Guide in Gettysburg, and graduated from Glassboro State College, Glassboro, New Jersey, in 1972. The author of many other works, including *Ready, Aim, Fire!*, *Cannons*, *An Introduction to Civil War Small Arms*, and *Percussion Ammunition Packets*, Dean is the leading authority on Civil War small arms ammunition. He is currently continuing work on the multi-volume *Round Ball to Rimfire: A History of Civil War Small Arms Ammunition*. The father of two children, Lauren and John, he founded Thomas Publications in 1981.

THOMAS PUBLICATIONS publishes books about the American Colonial era, the Revolutionary War, the Civil War, and other important topics. For a complete list of titles, please write to:

Thomas Publications,
P.O. Box 3031,
Gettysburg, PA 17325

Or visit our website:

www.thomaspublications.com

This book is intended for the growing number of bullet and cartridge collectors as a source of accurate and up-to-date information on bullets, cartridges and their manufacturers. It can also be used as a guide and checklist to help build a collection. It's the only source that fits in your pocket, so it can be easily carried and used at relic shows.

Based on field and archival research done in the past twenty-five years, we hope to correct some of the errors found in other works.

In this book we have attempted to illustrate, as much as practical, the variety of Civil War small arms ammunition. Bullets and cartridges are listed and followed by dimensions, weights and other available information. Any important variations are either shown or mentioned.

$9.95

ISBN 0-939631-94-6

YO-AVP-507